THE WAITING ROOM

Choosing To Thrive When Life Hurts

Dafnette D. Jones

xulon
PRESS

Table of Contents

To Jumaine:
Thank you for loving me unconditionally and remaining my faithful waiting room companion.

To my long-haul family and friends:
Thanks for your continued prayers and for encouraging me not to lose hope.

To Natasha:
I'm happy you chose to fight. I appreciate your compassionate support during a difficult time in your own life. I remain in awe.

Endorsements

"Many of us long for the Spirit of God to blow through our lives but find ourselves waiting in a mysterious stillness. Be encouraged. Dafnette Jones wrote this beautiful and powerful book for those of us who are waiting for the wind."

~**Ben Arment**, author of *Dream Year*

"Dafnette Jones' book, "The Waiting Room: How to Thrive When Life Hurts" is written with the sensitivity of someone who knows what it's like to be emotionally crushed, and the encouragement of a survivor of years of pain and disappointment. She not only weaves her own personal journey throughout the book with authenticity and transparency, but she threads the eternal hope of scripture throughout this great work as well; placing our lives against the backdrop of God's timeless truth in a way that is both therapeutic and thought provoking."

~**Keith Battle**, Lead Pastor, Zion Church in Largo, MD

"Whether single or married, with children or without, every woman has a desire that she secretly offers to God. In our hearts are the hidden things we long for and we often struggle with contentment and joy beyond the cliché of Christianity. This book offers a real look at one woman's experience and how she found encouragement, even in the waiting.

Dafnette reminds us that in the waiting, as Isaiah says, there is joy, strength and renewal. Welcome to the Waiting Room. There's something good for you here."

~**Jada Edwards**, Creative Arts Director,
One Community Church in Plano, TX

"Dafnette has a written an honest, thought-provoking, and emotionally captivating book about waiting. She addresses areas that some seek to avoid and aren't sure how to confront. This is a book for those who struggle in silence as they find themselves in waiting periods longer than anticipated. As Dafnette's husband, I know firsthand the challenges that we both face in the Waiting Room. I applaud her transparency and allowing God to use her by sharing her story with the world."

~**Jumaine Jones**, Lead Pastor of
The Bridge in Silver Spring, MD and author of
Lost In Love: Navigating the Five Relationship Terrains

"In The Waiting Room, Dafnette peels back the curtain to give us a raw, unfiltered, and engaging glimpse into the pain and confusion that sometimes comes with the mysterious ways and timing of God. With honesty and a rock-solid faith, she encourages readers to have the courage to make the kinds of choices that move us from being trapped in the grip of anger and cynicism to clinging to the grace and sovereignty of God— the one who is always good and faithful but at times confusing. With compassion and an intensely personal tone, Dafnette offers perspective and encouragement for those enduring the pain and disorientation of the waiting rooms of life and a blueprint for friends and family who have joined them there."

~**Heather Zempel**, Discipleship Pastor,
National Community Church in Washington, D.C.
and author of *Amazed and Confused*

"REAL Women sharing REAL life lessons excite me. I get giddy about it because too often women try to mask and cover how we really look and feel to impress the men AND the other women around us. Our pride often does not allow us to show any glimpses of our true selves, for fear someone will see a flaw in our facade. What Dafnette Jones has chosen to do in this book, The Waiting Room, is nothing short of revelatory. Her honest, raw, and transparent account of her journey leaves me inspired and challenged. For if she can experience, reflect on, and openly share such an intimately personal sojourn, surely I can be even more honest, transparent, and giving regarding my life's lessons. And the life lessons she lifts up in this account are so needed. For we all end up in a waiting room of some kind.

Dafnette not only shares with us WHAT we should choose to do while we wait but, through her own experiences, she shows us HOW to realistically live out those choices. I love that she does not shy away from the ugliness involved in waiting. Instead, she invites us to walk through the messiness and still come out on the other side with a greater awareness that no matter what the outcome, even if God does not grant me my heart's desire, I still have a responsibility to serve and produce.

I have several lines that stuck with me throughout my reading of Dafnette's book but so far, my favorite is, "No matter the outcome of my fertility journey, it can never be said that I failed to bear fruit." Indeed. This book, The Waiting Room, is just one of the countless fruit of her labor. Read and be blessed by it. I was."

~**Dr. Trenace Richardson**, REAL Women, Founder

INTRODUCTION

Not Our Choice

We've probably all had situations where we've had to wait for something – and not just while being in the waiting room of a business before our name is called for an appointment. Although this book focuses on my journey in waiting for children since marrying my husband, the journey started long before I wed. This is a winding journey that I believe you'll be able to relate to, even if your wait may be for something different.

I'll start with the backstory. Since youth, I looked forward to getting married and having children, as many women do. But the first part – marriage – seemed impossible. As a teenager and young adult, whenever a male with shared beliefs and values showed interest, I started envisioning him as my husband. I imagined our married lives and the children we'd have. But after four years of high school and eventually four years of college, with only two dates and no romantic relationships, I became discouraged. Meanwhile, friends and siblings were in relationships and starting to get married. At the dawn of my graduate school career, I was on an emotional rollercoaster. It seemed like I was the "only" female to whom suitable men were not attracted. However, not too long after college, God, in His sovereignty, allowed me to meet my future husband, Jumaine, during the first semester of graduate school. When Jumaine and I met, I did not know we'd soon enter a courting relationship. As we spent more time together, my feelings for him secretly grew. Call me old fashioned, but I desired for him to initiate pursuit, which meant I experienced great angst before he eventually expressed his interest in me. We pursued a relationship. A few years later, we exchanged wedding vows. At that point, I thought that, for sure, the second part of my lifelong dream – having children – would soon be fulfilled.

Fast forward several years, and Jumaine and I still await children. By now, we truly feel like Abraham and Sarah. I say to myself, *Don't get your hopes up*. Notwithstanding, each month I anticipate confirmation that I'm pregnant.

One Christmas Eve not long ago, after having recovered from earlier surgeries related to my fertility challenges, I deeply hoped for a special holiday, birthday, or anniversary gift from God – in the form of a pregnancy or newborn. The holiday season reminded me that with Him nothing is impossible (Luke 1:37). My confidence in God's ability to do the miraculous caused my hopes and expectations to soar. I allowed my Christmas joy to hang on the possibility of much-anticipated good news. Imagine my grave disappointment when it became unmistakably clear that I was not pregnant. Although grateful for my Savior, I cried on Christmas. *Why now*? I asked. *Could my disappointment have been postponed until tomorrow? Why Christmas Eve? Why Christmas?*

This is just one example of the many ups and downs that I've had along my journey of desiring offspring – my longest, most difficult "waiting room," if you will. But I know my story is one of many. Maybe you too are waiting for the tide to turn in your life. Some married couples are wondering why unresolved conflicts persist in their marriages. Students hoping to advance or hold on to their scholarships wonder why, even after countless hours of study, they continue to perform poorly on exams. Graduates stand dismayed that, after investing significant sums of money into their education, they have yet to secure their dream job – let alone gainful employment. Dedicated employees cannot understand why they are constantly overlooked for promotions and remain at a standstill in their careers. Gifted artists wonder why they continue to live paycheck to paycheck.

This isn't the life we imagined. Occasional setbacks and disappointments are one thing — recurring hurdles another. The latter can render life seemingly unbearable. For those of us who call ourselves believers, or Christ-followers, it can be especially difficult when the unfulfilled desires we seek are those esteemed in Scripture and championed within our faith community. Most of us probably did not choose our present, tumultuous circumstance, yet here we sit. Here we worry. Here we cry.

When met with recurring disappointment, joy and contentment can become elusive. Moreover, processing life's grim realities threatens our productivity and ability to live fulfilling lives. After all, in an era marked by empiricism, even the devout believer in God may conclude that moving forward in hope is a futile endeavor. We ponder what to make of life's unrelenting challenges and how faith in God can withstand the crushing weight of disappointment and unfulfilled desires.

Ironically, it's when we're crushed that our true selves are exposed and the benefits of faith realized. What follows is my personal journey through disappointment. I share neither to merely vent nor to assign blame for my experiences. Rather, I write to share what I've learned in my waiting room and how I survive. I seek to encourage any who are hurting with the knowledge that they're not alone in their bitter musings and struggles when facing prolonged difficulty and unfulfilled expectations. I hope that all who feel crushed by life's challenges and uncertainties will be empowered and inspired to endure. While we may feel overlooked and alone in a particular waiting room, we're not. God knows we're here, and He's already attending to us. The choices we make now will determine the quality of our waiting room experience.

CHAPTER 1

Time-Conscious – *Choose To Thrive*

For as long as I can remember, I've watched the clock. I cared about it growing up, when I kept a busy schedule with rigorous college prep classes, activities at the church my father pastored, not to mention other extracurricular activities. I kept track of all these activities with a detailed daily schedule. When it came to projects and appointments, I wanted to know start times, end times, and due dates well in advance.

As years pass and my responsibilities increase, time remains a treasured commodity. I want neither to waste others' time nor have mine wasted. Moreover, the thought of keeping others waiting makes me anxious. Simply ask my husband who gets to witness my time-conscious fits firsthand. I seek to arrive at meetings and appointments on time, largely to avoid inconveniencing others and mindful of other things that I have to get to. When people entrust me with their time, I seek to ensure that their time is well spent. As a matter of fact, when planning events, I aim to start and finish as scheduled. Each moment is carefully thought out. I actually schedule wait times, transition times, and delay margins. Furthermore,

I like to keep things moving along. I value efficiency and don't like to spend more time than necessary on any item or point of action. I wish to respect and maximize others' time in the same way I like for others to respect my time.

I've also become increasingly aware that what's scheduled gets accomplished — to include leisure and quality time with others. If it's a priority, it gets scheduled. Because I put careful thought into my schedule and often make sacrifices to add things to my schedule, I'll admit I get frustrated when things knock me off course. – Have I provided sufficient information for you to assess my personality? If you know me well, you're probably snickering. — Yes it unsettles me when others are nonchalant regarding tardiness and fail to provide advance notice of delays for appointments and events that have a publicized or agreed upon start time, especially if I hurried to arrive on time. If there's a hold-up or delay, I want to know why. Moreover, I want to know when will things get moving? What's your estimated time of arrival?

My time-conscious nature means my patience is often tried when I arrive for scheduled doctor's appointments. I have hurried to appointments only to remain in the waiting room well beyond my scheduled appointment time. My temper rises when I have to wait fifteen minutes, thirty minutes, and sometimes more than an hour past the time arrived. Consternation settles on my face and I begin grumbling in my head when someone who arrives after me is called back to see the physician first. A great sense of injustice overcomes me. On some occasions, I bring my concern to receptionists' attention and diplomatically assert my right to be seen first. There's little I can say or do, however, when informed that the patient in with the doctor had a scheduled appointment that preceded mine. On some occasions, I receive no explanation as to why I'm still waiting beyond my scheduled appointment time. I'm simply informed that the physician will see me soon. Meanwhile, I watch as others are called back, and I wonder — will I be called next?

Maybe you can relate to this overwhelming sense of impatience and seeming injustice in other areas of life. You're the oldest child, yet your younger siblings got married before you. Even your nieces and nephews have families of their own. Maybe you and your spouse have tried to conceive for seven years, and your newlywed co-worker announces his wife's pregnancy during the staff retreat. You've played on the team for three years and the new recruit gets promoted to team captain. You have worked for the same company the past five years with neither a salary increase, nor a promotion. Watching the minutes, hours, days, seasons, and years go by heightens our frustration.

Sure there was a time when we didn't watch the clock or we looked at the calendar less intently. When we unhurriedly showed up to the doctor's office and had no pressing affairs to attend to afterward, it didn't ruffle our feathers when we learned that the doctor wouldn't see us right away. The first day on our new job, it didn't bother us that we weren't being considered for promotion. We were simply happy to be there. We were grateful for a job. We were grateful that we were able to get an appointment. Five months after the wedding, it didn't matter that we weren't expecting our first child. We were thrilled to be married. Somewhere along the way, our awareness changes. We pull out our watches. We start to look at the calendar. Sometimes we do this on our own. Sometimes, other people or unforeseen circumstances turn our attention to the clock.

I became most time-conscious when I learned that uterine fibroids were impacting my health and quality of life. This happened during my first year of marriage. Less than nine months after getting married, my husband and I didn't learn that we'd welcome our firstborn. Regrettably we learned that I needed surgery that would require my husband and me to wait a year to conceive a child. Thus, our gazes turned to the clock. Unbeknownst to me at the time, this discovery ushered in a now ten-year season of waiting — waiting in doctors' offices, waiting in recovery rooms, and waiting for a breakthrough.

Recovering from my first surgery, I decided to do a personal study of the Old Testament to examine how leaders' actions and the quality of their obedience to God impacted the people they led. One day, while the desire to have children weighed heavily on my heart, I read about the Shunammite woman in 2 Kings 4. The prophet, Elisha, encountered this woman while passing through the region of Shunem. Appreciative of her hospitality whenever he passed through the area, Elisha wanted to reward her. When Elisha's servant, Gehazi, shared that the Shunammite woman was childless, God's prophet responded by declaring she would have a son the following year.

The fact that I read beyond my intended stopping point that day is worth noting. I neither intended to read this passage nor recalled ever reading it before. While poring over verses 8-17, my recent surgery and concerns regarding my reproductive future suddenly came to mind, as well as a calm assurance that God was aware of my circumstances and desire. In these verses, the Shunammite woman received the unexpected news that she would conceive a child. Elisha's words caught me off guard just as they did the Shunammite woman. At that moment, I believe God affirmed that Jumaine and I would have children. God did not, however, lay out the details, nor did He specify when we would have children.

Rather than cling most to the perceived promise that we'd have children, my time-conscious mind focused on an assumed time frame in which I felt God would make offspring a reality: one year. After all, Elisha told the Shunammite woman, "At this season next year you will embrace a son." When my physician gave us the "all clear," I became eager to conceive. Despite knowledge that with the Lord one day is like a thousand years and a thousand years like one day (2 Peter 3:8), I anticipated having a baby the following year – in Summer 2007. My life-long desire to have children would then be realized – or so I thought.

Fast-forward nearly ten years. We're still waiting. My desire for offspring has proved one of my most elusive desires, and opened my eyes to certain misconceptions I had about life and how God is supposed to work in the lives of those who seek to obey Him.

A part of me no longer wants to anticipate being pregnant, while another part does. By a certain time each month, I reach for the pregnancy test. Each test has yielded negative results. Another month passes with no affirming baby news. As I wait, I become frustrated with myself for allowing my hopes to rise. Nothing changes.

To make matters worse, others are wounded by my deflated dream. Some months I eagerly tell my husband, Jumaine, that I passed my anticipated cycle start date and could be pregnant. Earlier in our journey he too outwardly shared my excitement. As time passes, however, he also has learned not to get his hopes up. At times I've even become upset that he fails to share my excitement or insists that I refrain from taking a pregnancy test. This has led to heated conversations, during which I've discovered that he's guarding his own emotions and seeking to protect me from inevitable disappointment. I've even learned that sometimes he does get excited, but refrains from articulating it. In response, I attempt to put on a good front for him when the telltale signs of my cycle commence. I hesitate to tell him that this isn't our month. I cry, "Please God, help me to keep it together. Help me to think about other things and to rejoice over Your many blessings." I feel as if I'm continuously set up for a letdown.

Passing time hasn't been the only deterrent to hope. Promising opportunities that end in disappointment also reduce one's hope quotient. Further, just when I've lost track of time, and think I'm in my "happy place," someone comes along to remind me that I'm on the waiting list. Another sonogram picture coupled with a pregnancy announcement appears on social media. Someone casually tells me it's backwards for my younger sibling to have children before I do. Why all of the reminders? Now I'm more hopeful, more anxious, more disappointed. Can you relate?

Need I mention the other contributing factors to my emotional roller coaster? Throughout the years, I've received calls from friends far away who've said that they had dreams of me being pregnant. One Sunday at church, a young man who had no knowledge of our earnest attempts to conceive came to my husband and me, saying, "God told me to tell you that I'll be a good babysitter." He said he didn't know why, but he felt led to tell us that. Co-workers have pulled me aside to inquire if I'm with child. Students asked. Curious folks have even asked relatives if I'm with child. Sucking in my midsection and making strategic wardrobe selections have yet to defuse curiosities, especially when I encounter people who haven't seen me for a while. As a matter of fact, one day I ran into a co-worker in the doctor's office. We were seeing the same physician. One of us came for a pre-natal visit, the other because of issues potentially hindering pregnancy. Can you guess which patient I was?

Even on vacation, wanting to get away from it all, I encounter reminders of my unmet desire. Holding on to small rays of hope, I exercise precaution when a spa warns against certain treatments if I may be pregnant. During one trip, I even took a pregnancy test to be on the safe side. The results devastated me and filled me with woe the remainder of the trip. What's more, while awaiting the return flight home, I received a call from a loved one sharing that she was pregnant. Countless stories like this fill my journey, and the emotional roller coaster has yet to end.

Yes, I'm still here. I remain in the waiting room, looking forward to my turn. I didn't expect to be here this long. *What's taking so long? Is there something wrong with me? Why are people who arrived after me being serviced first?* My smile and high hopes have been replaced with frustration and disappointment. Several times I thought that the door was opening for me. To my dismay, another couple, another woman, was called in ahead of me. What's going on? I arrived "on time." I followed the instructions given prior to arrival. Yet here I sit, waiting for ten years. I sit in the waiting room, wondering why my issue hasn't been attended to. I wonder when the Physician will attend to me. Why did He call me into to the waiting room long before He intended to see me? It doesn't seem fair. What makes others a higher priority than me?

In a sermon, Pastor Keith Battle rightly said, "God doesn't give numbers and status updates in the waiting room." He also added, "Arrival time doesn't indicate appointment completion time." My husband and I cannot explain why countless other couples have experienced the blessing of offspring while we continue to wait. Yet here we are, waiting and learning. I wish that I could say that I've always remained patient in the waiting room. But each day is different. Sometimes joy overshadows my disappointment. Other days, I'm filled with sorrow.

Four years into my wait, I found myself reading through the Old Testament again. Rachel's words in Genesis 30 struck a chord. She said to her husband Jacob, "Give me children or else I die" (Genesis 30:1). I can relate to Rachel's intense feelings. At times I've assigned the blame for my husband and me not conceiving children to potential inadequacies on my part. On other occasions, however, I wonder if my husband can do something more to improve our chances. After all, other women in my physical condition have conceived and borne children. Someone or something else beyond me must be to blame. The question remains: *Why haven't we borne offspring?*

Jacob's response to Rachel answers the question before me. "Am I in the place of God who has withheld from you the fruit of the womb?" (Genesis 30:2). While there may be physiological factors that contribute to our failure to produce offspring, God's sovereignty is ultimately at work. Whether my husband and I conceive is up to God. The challenge now is to accept God's sovereignty and trust that He cares. Herein lies the dilemma. Our all-powerful, loving God is presently withholding from us the fruit of the womb. It doesn't matter that He's allowed other couples to experience similar hardship, it's happening to me now, and it doesn't feel good. I cannot understand why things have worked out for others while I remain waiting and wanting. Moreover, any glimpse of hope is quickly shadowed by more disheartening news. It's becoming increasingly difficult to breathe. At times I feel as if I cannot go on. I cannot take another negative pregnancy test or another physician's grim prognosis.

Throughout my life, I often found hope in biblical affirmations that God answers prayers and that He gives us the desires of our heart. As I look back over my life, indeed some of my past desires and most fervent petitions have been granted. I graduated high school with honors. God provided funding for my undergraduate career. I had employment right out of college. When desiring to attend graduate school and searching for employment a year later, again God made provision at the eleventh hour. Not only did my position remain open, my employer also provided a new incentive that covered the cost of grad school. As these prayers were being answered, finally God opened doors for the special someone who would later become my husband to walk into my life. Granted, there were bumps along these journeys — many shed tears and numerous questions — but the grief experienced during those periods of waiting pale in comparison to the sorrow I have come to know as a married woman still seeking children.

Indeed, each season of life brings blessings and challenges. I wholeheartedly agree with a pastor who once commented that the blessings of God complicate our lives. It would seem that I had everything necessary to live life happily ever after. Well, with each new season come new dreams and aspirations. This journey opened my eyes to truths that are essential and strong enough to sustain others and myself through many of life's inevitable disappointments: childlessness, loss, financial struggles, prolonged illness, broken relationships, loneliness, and so forth. Thus, where I've been inclined to become a cynical Christian, I've become what I believe to be a more levelheaded person of faith. In the faith community, one may find levelheadedness and faith antithetical. These are not mutually exclusive ideals.

Faith means to trust and align our actions with belief that God is at work and that God will work things out for the best. Encouraging people to persevere and remain steadfast, the writer of Hebrews states that "faith is the assurance of things hoped for, the conviction of things not seen" (Hebrews 11:1). The writer goes on to state that without faith it is impossible to please God, for the person who comes to God must believe that God is and that He rewards those who seek Him (Hebrews 11:6). It's helpful to understand the context of Hebrews. Facing persecution and hardship, people contemplated abandoning faith in Christ and returning to former ways. This is the same group of people who at one point in time joyfully embraced hardship for the gospel (see Hebrews 10:32-34). In the preceding verses, the writer exhorts, "Therefore, do not throw away your confidence, which has a great reward. For you have need of endurance, so that when you have done the will of God, you may receive what was promised" (Hebrews 10:35-36). If you take time to read the Faith Hall of Fame enumerated in Hebrews 11, you'll find quite the passage of time and numerous encounters with hardship between promises and fulfillments. We aren't the first in history to consider abandoning our present course.

While faith compels us to move in the direction of an anticipated outcome, levelheadedness keeps us grounded. Levelheadedness involves both walking in faith and recognizing that I lack the power and capacity to either orchestrate or predict the details of the anticipated outcome. Accordingly, levelheadedness allows us to keep our composure when things don't go as we planned. Furthermore, I find that levelheadedness, accompanied by faith, drives me to grow, prosper, and serve others even when things don't unfold in the manner and time that I wish. I needn't live a fruitless life as I await what's coming.

My interactions with countless others reveal that I'm not alone in my sentiments. Sure, we recognize that life hasn't been entirely bad. We've experienced joy, success, deliverance, and answered prayers. Meanwhile, we want more. We want better. We desire the good things that Scripture talks about — peace, marriage, children, healing, prosperity, and deliverance. We're just waiting for our time, our opportunity. We're simply discouraged by the fact that we're still waiting. This is, however, where we must be most cautious. We must refrain from regarding our waiting season as a season of dormancy. We must aim to not only bide our time, we must choose to thrive. While seasons and times lie in God's hands, He's presently entrusted us with talents, abilities, and resources to use. Have you noticed that doctors' offices always provide something for us to do in the waiting room — read magazines, watch the news, etc.? It's possible for us to thrive, experience personal development, and make a positive impact on the world around us even when life is hardest. This requires that we resolve to spend more time using the tools and resources already in our hands and at our disposal than we spend watching the time. Time is in good hands — God's hands.

Psalm 31:14-15 – [14]But as for me, I trust in You, O Lord, I say, "You are my God." [15]My times are in Your hand…

CHAPTER 2

Angry With God – *Choose Reverence*

We experience a whirlwind of emotions when waiting. Throughout my life, my heart wept for people who unapologetically expressed that they were angry with God. Like me, have you wondered how someone could harbor such contempt toward a faithful, loving, and generous God? I sought to assuage the strong emotions that others possessed. In my infertility journey, however, eventually I became one of those despondent people whom I'd usually encourage to hang in there and keep the faith. I harbored anger and frustration toward the God I love.

I shocked myself, one of the days I became most angry. I drove home enraged, I vented my rant to my mother and, in the privacy of my own home, I let God have it. What upset me most this evening wasn't the fact that God had closed my womb. It enraged me that God repeatedly allowed salt to be added to existing wounds. Why such a low blow at an inopportune time?

Earlier that evening, I had left my home eager to spend time with my sister and a few close friends. I anticipated a carefree ladies night out. My sister and two friends had already gathered around a table when I arrived. We talked for a short while before others joined us. There, a friend whom I hadn't seen in a while shared that she was expecting. I had missed the baby bump, as she was seated when I arrived. With the exception of my sister, who knows me quite well, no one at the table knew that my heart sunk within.

For the rest of the evening, I tried to remain actively engaged in conversation. I even shared congratulatory words. All the while, I wondered why God allowed this to happen again. At that very moment, several women in my various circles were expecting children. Mindful of my vulnerability, why did I have to find out about my friend's pregnancy during our ladies night out, an evening when I wanted to forget about my troubles and just have a good time? I detested the reminder that God continues to bless other couples with off-spring while my husband and I continue praying and waiting. The whole scenario seemed cruel and unfair.

This had been a protracted season of praying for others who desired offspring and seeing God answer their prayers. As soon as I embraced the reality of rejoicing with other couples and felt I could breathe, another crushing blow came my way. It enraged me, knowing that the powerful God I served persistently elected to keep my womb closed. Thus, I attacked God for keeping my womb closed and failing to protect me from further sorrow. *Why was God intentionally blessing others and leaving my husband and me out? Why was God constantly placing us in a position to serve, equip and encourage individuals and couples whom He chose to give the very gift that we desire?* There was no escaping the reminder that our union had yet to produce offspring.

In time, my rage turned to tears. Despite not wanting to pray to the God who allowed me to experience such hurt, I knew deep within that God wasn't maliciously causing these painful episodes to occur in my life. But my stubborn spirit, feeling justified in its rage, didn't want to be comforted in this moment. I wanted my feelings to be acknowledged. I wanted to be heard and appeased. Yet, I prayed and, eventually, accepted God's comfort.

My overall posture toward God amid the incessant reminders of my unwelcome, static circumstances changed soon after revisiting the book of Job. In it, we learn that Job was a man of integrity who obeyed God and helped others, yet he faced undue hardship. He lost nearly everything. His children died. He lost his livestock and his livelihood. On top of that, he was stricken with poor health. This highly respected man had come to utter ruin. A few verses in Job give us insight into how he felt:

Job 30:20-21, 25-27
[20]"I cry out to You for help, but You do not answer me;
I stand up, and You turn Your attention against me.
[21]"You have become cruel to me;

With the might of Your hand You persecute me."
[25]"Have I not wept for the one whose life is hard?
Was not my soul grieved for the needy?
[26]"When I expected good, then evil came;
When I waited for light, then darkness came.
[27]"I am seething within and cannot relax;
Days of affliction confront me."

Job 31:3-4
[3]"Is it not calamity to the unjust
And disaster to those who work iniquity?
[4]"Does He not see my ways
And number all my steps?"

Job's sorrow and frustration are apparent. Facing one calamity after another, he pondered why God seemed unresponsive. Job deemed his circumstances unjust and poised himself to challenge God. As a matter of fact, Job's words express my own sentiments. I too am seething within and cannot relax.[1] Moreover, like Job, I don't feel I deserve the hardship that I face. In Job 31:35, Job continues his protest:

> "Oh that I had one to hear me!
> Behold, here is my signature;
> Let the Almighty answer me!"

As a child, my desired career path changed from being an artist and author to a lawyer. Claire Huxtable's character on the *Cosby* show may have had something to do with that. Although I ended up choosing another profession, even to this day, I like crafting solid arguments and seeing justice prevail. Despite my calm demeanor and reputed pleasantness, I will diplomatically argue a case that I feel strongly about. Like Job, I too have a case that I wish to be heard.

How many of us are preparing arguments right now and ready to meet God in court? We demand an explanation for why bad things are happening in our lives. We demand an immediate response and resolution. We want answers! We want change!

God responds to Job's accusation.

Job 40:1-2, 8-9 (NIV)

[1]The Lord said to Job:
[2]"Will the one who contends with the Almighty
correct him?
Let him who accuses God answer him!"

[8]"Would you discredit my justice?
Would you condemn me to justify yourself?
[9]Do you have an arm like God's,

and can your voice thunder like his?"

Job 41:11 (ESV)
"Who has first given to me, that I should repay him?
Whatever is under the whole heaven is mine."

In preceding verses, God reminds Job that He is Lord of
the universe. God sees, controls and governs things that we
cannot. Further, all that we will ever have comes from God.
God informs Job – and us, for that matter – that we're in no
position to argue with Him.

I, like Job, was convicted by God's response in Job 40:1-2,
8-9 and 41:11. In reply, Job humbly yields to God's providence and withdraws his complaint. We read in Job 42:1-6:

¹Then Job answered the Lord and said,
²"I know that You can do all things,
And that no purpose of Yours can be thwarted.
³'Who is this that hides counsel without
knowledge?'
Therefore I have declared that which I did not
understand,
Things too wonderful for me, which I did not know."

Job acknowledges God's power, and that His plans and
purposes cannot be prevented. Moreover, God's knowledge
and understanding transcend our own. He sees and knows
things that we do not. Thus, we're in a position to neither
instruct nor counsel God regarding our circumstances. Job
goes on to say:

⁴'Hear, now, and I will speak;
I will ask You, and You instruct me.'
⁵"I have heard of You by the hearing of the ear;

33

But now my eye sees You;
⁶Therefore I retract,
And I repent in dust and ashes."

Job submits to God's supreme authority and humbly repents for speaking out of line.

Although Job's circumstances didn't change then, his time in God's presence changed his perspective, enabling him to say, "Now my eye sees You."

We have to respect God's response to our requests, even when He says "no" or "wait." In their book discussing boundaries, Drs. Henry Cloud and John Townsend include a section examining God's relationship to our boundaries. They write, "In the same way that we want others to respect our no, God wants us to respect his. He does not want us to make him the bad guy when he makes a choice. We don't like others trying to manipulate or control us with guilt, and neither does he."[2] They also point out that, despite expressing his displeasure, Job still held God in high regard and refrained from withdrawing his love from God when angry. We must do likewise: accept God's decision — even when it's not the one we wanted – and maintain fellowship with Him.

In my current circumstances, God has brought both comfort and correction. It takes humility to receive both. For instance, I have to resist a pride that wants to wallow in self-pity, shouts what I deserve, and demands immediate gratification. I also must recognize that my accusations against God are illegitimate. While my feelings and emotions are quite real and worthy of recognition, any contempt toward God that my legitimate sorrow arouses must be checked. Moreover, I must humbly repent for contemptuous words and feelings I hurl toward God.

As I unleash raw, unrestrained emotions, God reveals my own error and need for repentance. Time and again, I find that moments of intense sorrow and rage illuminate sin in my heart and character imperfections that may have otherwise gone unnoticed. Although I recognize and accept that I'm not perfect and will continue to fall short, I strive to be a "good person." Furthermore, there are certain undesirable traits that I strive to steer clear of, such as pride and jealousy. I now recognize that even "nice" people are vulnerable to pride and envy. Romans 3:23 informs us that all have sinned and fall short of the glory of God. Use of "fall" in the present tense indicates that we continue to come short of God's standard. This journey continues to reveal where I fall short.

Although my outward actions aren't usually cloaked in pride, my inward musings are. There were periods when my initial response to pregnancy announcements was, *"Why them and not* me?" Knowing full well that I'm no better than anyone else, moments still arose when I compared myself to others and concluded that I deserved certain blessings more than them. As a matter of fact, much of my anger toward God stemmed from the feeling that He's intentionally withholding something that I deserve — children. After all, I practiced abstinence while unmarried. My husband and I seek to be obedient to Scripture, and our lives are consumed by ministering to others.

I recently told someone, "Comparisons tend to breed sorrow." This is especially true during seasons of heartache and protracted disappointment. Besides generating sorrow, comparisons fertilize seeds of envy and discontentment. According to *Dictionary.com*, envy is a feeling of discontentment or covetousness regarding another's advantages, success, possessions, etc. In the same vein, jealousy is a feeling of resentment because of another's success or advantage. Finding myself cringing at the sight of pregnant women, strangers whose stories I did not know, alerted me to something ugly within. That I resented the fact that couples married fewer years than my husband and me continued to share pregnancy announcements also pointed to the deep-rooted bitterness and envy within. That I remained kind and supportive of the pregnant women whom I encountered or whose pregnancy photos I observed on social media was more a testament to divine empowerment to behave rightly than a pure heart. God continues to temper my emotions and help me overcome unbecoming predispositions of the flesh. As God exposes pride, envy, and discontentment in my heart, the sanctifying work of the Holy Spirit begins. As He changes me, my character becomes increasingly aligned with God's standards of goodness.

Like Job, I had to come to the realization that God owes me nothing. That I'm in good health, have more possessions than I can use in a week, and have the cognitive abilities to write this narrative are blessings beyond measure. None of us "deserve" the blessings and privileges that God bestows. Further, it's quite arrogant to minimize the experiences of others. We all have a story to tell.

Throughout the past ten years, numerous women have shared their concerns and challenges regarding conception. Many have requested my prayers and support, which I've willingly given. God has provided me with the capacity to empathize with others. I have shared other women's burdens and fervently petitioned God on their behalf. I've gone as far as to say, "Lord, even if it means blessing them with children before You bless me, please allow them to conceive and bear offspring." Time and time again, I've seen my request answered.

As time passes, women continue to solicit my prayers and support during challenging fertility and pregnancy journeys. While I continue to pray for them, I must admit that I can no longer include the clause, "even if it means You bless them first." That's because it is increasingly difficult to see God move on behalf of others while I remain waiting. For those of you who beat yourself up because your resolve seems to weaken rather than strengthen over time, it may be freeing to know that, for some of us, things do not become easier over time. Rather, we become better prepared and more equipped to withstand the likely blows. Put another way, comparable to lifting weights, it's my observation that increased muscle mass and strength don't lighten one's burden. Rather, increased strength renders the burden more manageable. We can lift the load with a diminished threat of severe injury. Accordingly, I've learned to pray, "Please strengthen my heart and keep me from becoming consumed with disappointment and envy if You choose to bless them first." This is what I like to call "preemptive prayer." While this doesn't take away the pain, it buffers the impact and secures my footing.

You may agree that it's easy to rejoice with others when things are going well in your own life. Surely, the instruction in Romans 12:15, to rejoice with those who rejoice, becomes increasingly difficult when repeatedly seeing people receive the very things for which you've been praying. I've asked, "Lord, please help me to endure this season." Several times I thought that I was coming out of this barren period only to be met with disappointment. Although my hope in God remains because I know His promises are true, the repeated disappointment remains difficult to endure. Thus, I also continually pray, "Lord, please help me to stay strong as I encounter and celebrate other expectant mothers. Help me to treat people the same way that I want to be treated. Help me to rejoice with those who rejoice." You may have to ask God to empower you to celebrate the friend who recently purchased a new home; the co-worker who received a pro-motion; the roommate who just got engaged; the organiza-tion that's experiencing exponential growth; the artist whose career swiftly takes off; or the spokesperson whose platform continues to increase.

Scripture exposes sin, mindsets and practices that fall short of God's standards, and sin's destructive results. Scripture also equips us to overcome sin. I take to heart biblical warnings such as James 3:16: "For where jealousy and selfish ambition exist, there is disorder and every evil thing." Not only does it matter to me that envy displeases God, but because I abhor evil and desire peace with others, I must put off envy. When I do, I'm able to love and enjoy pleasant relationships with people who have specific "advantages" and opportunities that I desire. I also recognize that pride holds the capacity to deteriorate the relationships I cherish. Moreover, pride will either strip away my ability to leverage the influence God has given me for good, or cause me to forsake the opportunities for personal growth and greater impact that arise. After all, the countless insecurities magnified by my fertility challenges are essentially outgrowths of pride. I cannot bear failing to measure up to the standards imposed most often by myself – by others, less often. Perhaps pause and take a few minutes to digest the preceding sentence.

When angry with God and His providence, it's easy to begin attacking His character and to shun His presence. In addition, we may begin to question the utility of our devotion. Even in Scripture, we see where one worshiper and temple musician, Asaph pondered:

Psalm 73:12-14 (ESV)
[12]Behold, these are the wicked;
always at ease, they increase in riches.
[13]All in vain have I kept my heart clean
and washed my hands in innocence.
[14]For all the day long I have been stricken
and rebuked every morning.

When we continue reading Psalm 73, we learn that Asaph's bitter musings changed when he came into God's presence (verses 16-17). God changed Asaph's perspective, causing him to both repent and recognize God's goodness.

Psalm 73:21-26 (ESV)

[21]When my soul was embittered,
when I was pricked in heart,
[22]I was brutish and ignorant;
I was like a beast toward you.
[23]Nevertheless, I am continually with you;
you hold my right hand.
[24]You guide me with your counsel,
and afterward you will receive me to glory.
[25] Whom have I in heaven but you?
And there is nothing on earth that I desire besides
you.
[26] My flesh and my heart may fail,
but God is the strength of my heart and my portion
forever.

No matter how low I feel, I am quickly reminded that I must still honor and respect God. This truth brings to mind my teen years. No matter how upset I became over the rules and restrictions my parents set, I knew there would be consequences if I communicated my displeasure in a disrespectful manner. In many households, children dare not overtly indicate that they disagree with their guardians. But God graciously allows us to bring our petitions, concerns, and disappointments to Him. As a matter of fact, He wants us to. God's word instructs us to cast our cares on Him because He cares for us (1 Peter 5:7). That God allows room for us to vent our sorrows and disappointments does not, however, diminish His authority. Neither does this liberty God affords mean that He will be amenable to all of our petitions. He will, however, hear them and provide the best response at the appropriate time.

It's important to get before God no matter what we're going through. When we become consumed with anger toward God and bitterness regarding our circumstances, we become less eager to remain in God's presence. We may not want to pray to Him or read Scripture. However, continuing to get closer to God is the key to enduring and ultimately overcoming life's seeming setbacks. Again, I emphasize that it requires great humility to exchange our will for God's solace and providence – a battle indeed. Not only do we have to rise above our own emotions, there are other forces at play, steering us away from fellowship with God. As we pour out our hearts to God, He reveals Himself to us and we, too, begin to see Him for the mighty, all-knowing God He truly is.

Further, as we study Scripture, we receive timely reminders of God's faithfulness, goodness, and love. Here are a few reminders that provide me divine attitude adjustments as I await God's ultimate resolution:

Psalm 103:2 – Bless the LORD, O my soul, And forget none of His benefits...

James 5:11 – We count those blessed who endured. You have heard of the endurance of Job and have seen the outcome of the Lord's dealings, that the Lord is full of compassion and is merciful.

Deuteronomy 2:7 (ESV)–For the Lord your God has blessed you in all the work of your hands. He knows your going through this great wilderness. These forty years the Lord your God has been with you. You have lacked nothing.

Hebrews 12:1-2 (ESV)–[1]Therefore, since we are surrounded by so great a cloud of witnesses, let us also lay aside every weight, and sin which clings so closely, and let us run with endurance the race that is set before us, [2]looking to Jesus, the founder and perfecter of our faith, who for the joy that was set before him endured the cross, despising the shame, and is seated at the right hand of the throne of God.

As we stay in God's presence, we gain unimaginable strength to live productive, God-honoring lives even when met with recurring disappointment. God's presence and word comfort us, strengthen our resolve, and assuage our anger.

The God who governs the universe, forgives our transgressions, provides for our needs, renews our strength, and restores our joy deserves reverence always. Our circumstances diminish neither His grandeur nor His goodness. While waiting, may our anger and contempt give way to reverence and devotion as we humbly run to God.

Job 6:10 – "But it is still my consolation, And I rejoice in unsparing pain, That I have not denied the words of the Holy One."

CHAPTER 3

Overcoming Cynicism – *Choose Hope*

*O*ver time, I've come to take lightly Scripture passages suggesting that God fulfills desires. This is because over time, I have become hurt and embittered by the fact that some of my desires remain unfulfilled. Scriptures such as Psalm 37:4 state, "Delight yourself in the Lord; And He will give you the desires of your heart." Albeit, I know full well that this Scripture doesn't guarantee that God will give me everything that I want, and concede that some things I formerly desired, if placed in my hands, would prove disadvantageous to myself, and potentially harmful to others. This passage does, however, inform us that we can trust God to accomplish God-honoring desires that align with His righteous purposes.

Meanwhile, my desires have yet to be fulfilled. It's not that I no longer believe these passages that inspire hope to be true. I simply believe that I'm the exception. That is, I believe that these great moves of God and welcome answers to prayer are reserved for others. Thus, other women can rightly echo Hannah's words – "for this *child* I prayed, and the LORD has given me my petition which I asked" (1 Samuel 1:27). Rather than focusing on God's power to perform fertility miracles, I regard the accounts of barren women such as Sarah, Rachel, Hannah, and the Shunammite woman as nice accounts of how God moved on behalf of another. There was a time, however, when I was most inclined to be encouraged that God can and will move on my behalf, just as He did for them. Nevertheless, as time progresses and I see this miracle extended to others, I've felt that baby blessings just don't happen to me. Because of this one unmet desire, I found myself taking lightly any suggestion that God satisfies my desires. I allowed one disappointment to be my determining factor when it comes to God's ability to accomplish good things in my life.

To sum up my attitude, I allowed disappointment to render me cynical. Thus, I became distrustful of God's intentions and pessimistic toward His promises. We become vulnerable to bitterness and cynicism when we reduce God's character to the sum of one unfulfilled desire. After all, even in our waits we can point to other desires that God has satisfied. I'm reminded that God provided for me to attend grad school debt-free. Shortly after beginning grad school, I met a godly man, to whom I'm now married. Fast forward a few years and God provided a more spacious home. God even fulfilled my desire to attend seminary. Clearly, God satisfies my desires. This truth cannot be ignored as I face the one, two, or three other unmet desires. With this in mind, I can read the words of Scripture intended to encourage and allow them to strengthen my faith in God's good intentions for my life.

That I'm inclined to forget and lose sight of God's goodness and past blessings amid current hardships and disappointments makes it clearer why, countless times, God calls His followers to remember what He has done. 1 Chronicles 16:12 instructs those who seek God to "remember His wonderful deeds which He has done, His marvels and the judgments from His mouth." Similarly, the psalmist wrote, "Bless the LORD, O my soul, and forget none of His benefits" (Psalm

103:2). In another psalm reflecting Israel's history, we read, "Seek the Lord and His strength; seek His face continually. Remember His wonders which He has done, His marvels and the judgments uttered by His mouth" (Psalm 105:4-5). Additionally, I recall Joshua 4. God instructed His followers to take twelve stones from the middle of the Jordan River and to set them up at Gilgal as a perpetual reminder of what God did. He cut off the flowing waters of the Jordan, allowing the people to cross safely en route to the Promised Land. God said to the sons of Israel, in Joshua 4:21-24:

> When your children ask their fathers in time to come saying, 'What are these stones?' then you shall inform your children, saying, 'Israel crossed this Jordan on dry ground.' For the LORD your God dried up the waters of the Jordan before you until you had crossed just as the Lord your God had done to the Red Sea, which He dried up before us until we had crossed; that all the peoples of the earth may know that the hand of the Lord is mighty, so that you may fear the Lord your God forever.

When we fail to remember all God has allowed us to accomplish and the numerous blessings that He's given, we're most susceptible to grumbling and making harmful decisions. We see this throughout Scripture. You may be familiar with the account of God delivering the Israelites from Egyptian captivity. Despite ongoing displays of God's faithfulness and provision, the Israelites continued to grumble. Moses even informed the people that although they expressed their complaints to Moses, they were really grumbling against God. For instance, within a short while of God's miraculous provision of food, the Israelites' immediate response to failing to find water at their new campsite was to quarrel with Moses and test God (Exodus 17:1-3). The congregation went so far as to say, "Why, now have you brought us up from Egypt to kill us and our children and our livestock with thirst?" Scripture also informs us that they tested God, saying, "Is the LORD among us, or not?" Millennia later, we wonder how the Israelites doubted God, their deliverer. The psalmist describes the Israelites' forgetfulness and subsequent rebellion in Psalm 106:7:

> Our fathers in Egypt did not understand Your wonders;
> They did not remember Your abundant kindnesses,
> But rebelled by the sea, at the Red Sea.

Not only do we see where situational myopia causes us to forget God's goodness, failure to regard God's faithfulness and continued provision leads to sin and unrest. We see this in Scripture, throughout history, and in our own lives. When God doesn't come through for us in the exact manner we want, we tend to take situations into our own hands. We concoct plans to get what we want sooner and by nearly any means necessary. Against wise counsel, we exhaust our savings, incur debt, abandon our commitments, and at times blatantly disobey God. Even when we act contrary to our better judgment and wise counsel, we seek to justify our actions, assuming the end justifies the means. Proverbs 21:2 rightly observes, "Every man's way is right in his own eyes, But the LORD weighs the hearts."

Establishing our own memorial stones will help us remember God's mighty deeds in our lives. Following answered prayers and amazing feats that God accomplishes, we should set aside an item that reminds us of these respective incidents. This can be a photo, object, clothing article, newspaper clipping, video, and so forth. Although I have yet to bear offspring, I keep pictures of the fibroids removed during two surgical removals of uterine fibroids, myomectomies.

This may gross some out, but I'm a biology enthusiast. Need I mention, I requested to see the removed fibroids? To my dismay, I couldn't. However, my photos of them remind me that, despite the removal of numerous fibroids and excessive blood loss, God preserved both my uterus and my life.

My personal study and reflection on Scripture often leads me to Romans 8:28. It says, "And we know that God causes all things to work together for good to those who love God, to those who are called according to His purpose." I've read this verse numerous times. It often challenges me to look forward, trusting that God is working things out for the best. One particular day, however, yielded another challenge. As I focused on the words "and we know," I was challenged to reflect on what God has already accomplished. The declaration "and we know" suggests that those to whom Paul wrote already knew that God causes things to work together for the good of those who love God and are called according to His purpose. Thus, the verse compels us to recount prior experiences. We can find hope in the waiting room by recalling how God has allowed things to work out for the best in the past.

As I contemplated this insight, I recalled another period of uncertainty that I faced several years ago. When I graduated from college, I accepted a one-year teaching internship. At the end of the program, all interns were required to seek employment elsewhere, as it was not the school's custom to rehire interns the following year. Despite the favor I received from colleagues and everyone's high hopes for my future placement, I was turned down for several positions. I recall the great disappointment and embarrassment I felt as I prepared to inform my division head and supervising teacher that I received another rejection notice.

One morning, after sharing the disappointing news regarding another denial, I became surprised by the pleasant looks and non-verbal exchange between my division head and supervising teacher. My recent letdown positioned me for an invitation to remain with my current employer while pursuing a graduate degree at my employer's expense. This provided an answer to two prayers: obtaining employment and fulfilling my desire to pursue a master of education degree, which I had planned to defer due to limited financial resources and potentially having to relocate. God allowed me to gain invaluable experience that prepared me for future interviews, built my character and awareness of His faithfulness, and prevented me from walking through the wrong doors (at the time, I was inclined to walk through the first open door). He was at work, paving a better, more desirable path, for which I remain grateful.

It's true. I possess both intellectual and experiential knowledge of Romans 8:28. Nevertheless, the truth contained in it is still difficult to recognize when I'm consumed by disappointment over God's timing. I continually need God's strength and a firm grasp on the truth that He's at work. I'll be happiest in the end if I trust God, allowing Him to accomplish His purpose. After all, the passage reads that He causes things to work together for the good of those who love Him and are called according to His purpose. Complete surrender to God's divine intentions characterizes those who love Him and have submitted to His purpose.

In addition to having visual reminders of God's blessings, we should testify, or proclaim, these aloud. This is especially helpful when we cannot see God's hand in our current circumstances. Psalm 145, a psalm of praise, captures the sentiments and activity that will change our perspective when we become disillusioned and void of hope. For example, verses 6-7 say:

> [6]Men shall speak of the power of Your awesome acts,
> And I will tell of Your greatness.
> [7]They shall eagerly utter the memory of Your abundant goodness
> And will shout joyfully of Your righteousness.

When we recount God's goodness, it encourages us — and others.

Another exercise that helps me to rebound from downward spirals and negative musings regarding my current plight is to make a gratitude list. Someone recommended this exercise to me when it seemed God was answering everyone's prayers except mine. I became consumed by what God seemed to be withholding, rather than recognizing what He was giving. Whenever I start my list, one or two items immediately come to mind. As I write, even more things come to my attention. At the end of this exercise, I end up thanking God rather than sneering at Scripture's lofty promises.

Cultivating an attitude of gratitude will enhance our view of God and strengthen our resolve to honor Him. We must consider all areas of our life and acknowledge God's hand of blessing and provision. We should regularly take time to identify and record the things for which we're thankful. Most importantly, we should regularly take time to convey our gratitude. Praising God not only gives God the glory that He's due, it also illuminates His goodness and brightens the dark moments we face.

It's helpful to recognize when our thoughts become filled with cynicism and bitterness. Left unchecked, we're inclined to make rash, emotional decisions that we may later regret. If you're like me, your journey has taken you on an emotional roller coaster of highs and lows. We know firsthand that there are moments when we rebound and when we're genuinely happy. As a result, we must remember that even moments of sorrow will pass. God will renew our strength (Isaiah 40). Making wise, God-honoring decisions when we're sad will allow us to thrive not only in our sorrow, but also during sustained periods of joy.

When sorrow breeds anger, cynicism, or sin, the temptation is to keep these thoughts and actions to oneself. Both acknowledging and sharing our thoughts and shortcomings, however, is essential to moving forward and overcoming the gloom that we ultimately seek to escape. Foremost, we should share our thoughts, feelings, and actions with God. God welcomes us to cast our cares on Him. As we openly share our feelings with God, He exposes transgressions that may escape our notice. Accordingly, we must take the next step of confessing our sins to God. 1 John 1:9 (KJV) says that if we confess our sins, God is faithful and just to forgive them and cleanse us from all unrighteousness. Furthermore, the LORD can sympathize with our struggles. Hebrews 4:15 explains that "we do not have a high priest who cannot sympathize with our weaknesses, but One who has been tempted in all things as we are, yet without sin." The following verse says, "Therefore let us draw near with confidence to the throne of grace, so that we may receive mercy and find grace to help in time of need." I remain both amazed and grateful for God's grace and forgiveness when I attack His character and fail to trust Him. He's truly slow to anger and abundant in unfailing love, forgiving iniquity and transgression (Numbers 14:18). We can also learn from David's example in Psalm 32:1-5:

> ¹How blessed is he whose transgression is forgiven,
> Whose sin is covered!
> ²How blessed is the man to whom the Lord does not impute iniquity,
> And in whose spirit there is no deceit!
> ³When I kept silent about my sin, my body wasted away
> Through my groaning all day long.
> ⁴For day and night Your hand was heavy upon me;
> My vitality was drained away as with the fever heat of summer. Selah.
> ⁵I acknowledged my sin to You,
> And my iniquity I did not hide;

I said, "I will confess my transgressions to the
Lord";
And You forgave the guilt of my sin. Selah.

Not only will God forgive us, He also stands poised to
strengthen and comfort us. According to Psalm 55:22, when
we cast our burden upon the Lord, He will sustain us. Peter
also writes that we are to cast our anxieties on God because
He cares for us (1 Peter 5:7). Additionally, Philippians 4:6-7
informs us that, rather than being consumed by anxiety, we
are to pray and let our requests be made known to God. When
we cast our cares on God, He grants us peace that transcends
human understanding. Moreover, God will guard our hearts
and minds. I can attest to the fact that moments with God
when I've cried and poured out all that filled my heart and
mind have ended in an indescribable sense of peace and comfort. I no longer wanted to scream, and in some instances
abandoned musings that life wasn't worth living if filled with
such sorrow and recurring disappointment.

When getting before God, not only must we seek forgiveness, it's also imperative that we ask Him to fill us with more
of His Spirit. After all, when we walk in the power of the
Holy Spirit, we can avoid carrying out the inclinations of the
flesh such as idolatry, immorality, strife, jealousy, outbursts
of anger and drunkenness (Galatians 5:16-21). When filled
with the Spirit, we're able to exhibit love, joy, peace, patience,
kindness, goodness, faithfulness, gentleness, and self-control
(Galatians 5:22-23). Furthermore, self-awareness remains
important. The Holy Spirit helps facilitate self-awareness.
Allow God to search your heart and bring heart issues to the
forefront. Then seek His help to change. This may keep us
from acting on negative emotions and making decisions that
we later come to regret. Moreover, this may alert us to the
need to hold our tongue to preserve relationships and avoid

personal character assassination. We may also avoid false assumptions that stem from hurt.

In addition to confessing our sins to God and seeking more of His power, it's also important to share our struggles with others. James 5:16 instructs Christ-followers to confess our sins to one another, and pray for one another so that we may be healed. The Greek term translated *healed* has the idea of being made whole, or free from sin and error.[3] Galatians 6:1-2 states, "if anyone is caught in any trespass, you who are spiritual, restore such a one in a spirit of gentleness; each one looking to yourself, so that you will not be tempted. Bear one another's burdens, and thereby fulfill the law of Christ." This passage indicates that we must solicit the support of fellow believers when we struggle with sin. God intends for us neither to face nor overcome our sin issues alone. These verses also indicate that we're all vulnerable to sin. As a result, we should be able admit our shortcomings, and there should be trustworthy people poised to pray for us and help us bear our burdens in a God-honoring manner.

I'm grateful for the trusted friends whom God has placed in my life. I can be honest with them about my pride, bitterness, and envy. My transparency has allowed others to get in my corner and pray specific prayers regarding issues that have impacted me most, and threatened to lead me down a destructive path. These friends have permission to ask the tough questions. They can ask how I'm doing and how I feel about another's good news without me ever questioning their motives. Interestingly enough, some of those asking how I'm doing follow up with me as they enjoy their own pregnancies and motherhood. Just because some people have what I desire, or may not be able to relate to what I'm going through to the fullest extent, doesn't diminish their ability to listen, pray for, and encourage me.

Some of the factors rendering me comfortable sharing my deepest struggles include a person's trustworthiness, consistency, responsiveness, and genuine concern. Furthermore, I value the encouragement of others who are students of God's word, understand His character, are confident in the power of prayer, and are able to point me to biblical truth when despair impairs my vision. These are friends who call me or follow up the next day when they've witnessed someone utter an insensitive comment or share news that they know is likely to arouse sorrow, even if I'm able to maintain my game face in the moment.

I have opened up with friends about my struggle with pride and envy. Through a recent small group study, the Holy Spirit brought to my attention that my fertility journey also is tainted by failure to forgive. More specifically, I have kept a record of wrongs. According to 1 Corinthians 13:5, love keeps no record of wrongs. Accordingly, I recently shared with trusted friends that I'm praying that I resist harboring bitterness and entertaining contemptuous thoughts toward people who have solicited my prayers during their conception and pregnancy journey, but fail to initiate reaching out to me as my journey continues, or fail to express that they're likewise praying that God blesses my husband and me with offspring too. Albeit, some will share that they pray God will strengthen me and keep me from becoming overcome with sorrow, and they pray for my capacity to accept God's will. It can be difficult to oblige others' specific prayer requests when it seems they aren't continuing to oblige mine. The Lord provided this insight and revealed a hidden area in which I harbor an unloving disposition. The revelation drove me to pray that I'll let these unmet expectations go and continue to pray specific prayers for others without requiring it of them. It also prompted feedback from friends, who reminded me that even well-intentioned people may fall short of my expectations. Not to mention, I may fail to meet their expectations. Furthermore, a friend reminded me that with new responsibilities come new priorities that may understandably remove my husband and me from the forefront of people's minds. The Lord has also impressed on my heart that it's difficult for some to truly understand how I feel and, in an effort to help me or protect me from further disappointment, some may choose silence rather than the sincere, specific gestures of encouragement that I seek.

When God and friends align to encourage and hold me accountable, it protects me from sinful and unhealthy thought patterns and actions that will ultimately lead to diminished joy and disunity. Furthermore, God has allowed faithful friends and confidants to serve as His vessels, steering me away from hopelessness.

Happy "endings" exist. We can see the goodness of the Lord in the land of the living (Psalm 27:13). We must not allow our present disappointments and inability to see the future outcome of our present circumstances lead us away from God and toward unwise decisions. When we fail to recognize that God is truly near to the brokenhearted and saves those who are crushed in spirit (Psalm 34:18), we run the risk of making emotional decisions that fail to produce lasting relief, and potentially cause more harm than good. God really does care and His good intentions extend to all. Each day presents both a new opportunity and challenge to avoid further sin, and to keep the faith. Consider Hebrews 10:23: "Let us hold fast the confession of our hope without wavering, for He who promised is faithful." When we consider the surrounding verses, we find the passage encourages the saints to refrain from wavering and falling back into pre-conversion habits. Met with opposition, unmet desires, and discouragement, it may be easy to fall into unhealthy and ungodly habits. Remaining hopeful and trusting God's intentions is essential to walking in obedience to God and overcoming cynicism.

Again I'll admit that recurring disappointment has a way of diminishing one's hope quotient and causing one to question the utility of faith. What's more, we tire of getting our hopes up only to encounter further hardship. You too may wonder, is it possible to have "sober hope" — hope that's not vulnerable to recurring disappointment? This is one of the questions with which I wrestle most. While I lack the answer to that question, I have concluded that hope and disappointment aren't mutually exclusive. That is, disappointment is intrinsic to life under the sun, life on earth. Life under the lordship of the Son, Jesus Christ, however, assures us that our present hardships are only temporary. Our present disappointments pale in comparison to the glory that awaits us. As a matter of fact, even if the possessions, achievements, and aspirations we seek come to fruition, these are also temporary. While we cannot foresee the specific outcome of each challenge we face, God's word reveals the totality of life in Christ – everlasting satisfaction, joy, and peace. When we embrace hope in Christ and God's eternally good intentions, our capacity to thrive improves.

Psalm 119:143 — Trouble and anguish have come upon me, Yet Your commandments are my delight.

You Will Always Be

Who do I love most?
For You will always be.
What do I love most?
For You will always be?

Who do I want most?
For You will always be.
What do I want most?
For You will always be?

What does Your word esteem most?
For You will always be.

Neither marriage, nor children, nor status, nor wealth;
For You will always be.

Who died for me at Calvary?
Yes, You will always be.
Who restores my soul and makes me whole?
Yes, You will always be.

Fixing my eyes on Jesus, the author and perfecter of faith
Yes, You will always be.
For the joy set before You, You endured the cross, despising
the shame
Yes, You will always be.

You sit at the right hand of the throne of God.
Yes, You will always be.
I will not grow weary and lose heart,
For You will always be.

May I love you most
For You will always be.
May I want You most
For You will always be

You are mine
Yes, You will always be.
I am Yours
For You will always be.

CHAPTER 4

Love Misconceptions –
Choose To Fight

*I*n the preceding chapter, we acknowledged the reality of cynicism. Cynicism can ultimately be traced back to misconceptions regarding God's love and sovereignty. Having faced the same grim circumstances for nearly ten years, it becomes difficult to believe that things will ever change. Having walked alongside others through their brief stints in my situation, only to be left standing in the dust as doors opened for them to walk into their dreams of parenthood, I began to question why God seemingly had greater regard for others. Because I had seen God overwhelmingly grant other people's petitions for the same thing while I remained wanting, I perceived that God loved me less. I wondered what made others more special and worthy of God's special favor than me.

I couldn't understand why nearly every woman who had solicited my prayers as they pursued motherhood celebrated pregnancies and births within the span of a year. Couple after couple testified of God's goodness and how blessed the gift of offspring was. Meanwhile, my husband and I did not receive the same highly esteemed gift. I pondered why God chose to answer the burning desires and prayers of other women and couples, yet He had not removed our fertility challenges.

Although my inability to conceive and bear offspring had already aroused great insecurity and diminished my feelings of self-worth, these occurrences made matters worse. Fully aware that it was dangerous to make comparisons and that everyone had a story, my logical brain still instinctively processed and analyzed the empirical data it received. Based on my observations, I concluded that other women to whom God granted the privilege of motherhood were more special than me. Amid grave disappointment, I failed to realize that observations from which I drew my conclusions were far from objective. After all, my observations were filtered through my wavering emotions, predetermined assumptions, personal biases, and selfish motives. I drew conclusions about God's love based on subjective data.

Aware that I struggled to see God's love beyond the looming cloud of despair, for a period of time I programmed a calendar alert, stating, "God loves me and He's always good to me." Otherwise, I would continue to embrace the myth that I was unloved and good things happened to other people but not me. Further, biblical passages such as Psalm 139 reminded me of God's intimate care for everyone. Verses 17-18 declare, "How precious also are Your thoughts to me, O God! How vast is the sum of them! If I should count them, they would outnumber the sand. When I awake, I am still with You." Not only is God presently thinking of me, He also saw my unformed body and skillfully formed me in my mother's womb. That I have naturally occurring challenges to childbearing does not render me an inferior woman. It was a part of God's tailor-made plan for my life.

This holds true for all. As Psalm 139:14 reminds us, we are wonderfully made; wonderful are God's works. None of us is an afterthought. God loves you just as much as He loves me. God loves me as much as He loves you. God loves those of us who are waiting for things we desire just as much as He loves the people who possess the things that we want. They're not more special than we are. Moreover, we're neither more special, nor more entitled than they are.

Throughout this journey, well-intentioned people have suggested that my circumstances haven't changed because God is trying to teach me something, or because He still has to work on me. The problem with this line of reasoning is that it also arouses feelings of unworthiness and magnifies Satan's lie that "there is something wrong with me." It unsettles the otherwise upstanding person who strives to live with integrity and devotion to God, and communicates, "You're not good enough yet." Furthermore, this line of reasoning implies that God's love and kindness are granted based on merit. This suggests that we receive blessings from God once we're worthy. The truth is there are lessons to learn and growth that needs to take place both while waiting and as we enjoy God's blessings. Nevertheless, it's unwise to conclude that we remain in our current state of want because we have yet to meet an elusive standard. Moreover, this line of reasoning is antithetical to grace.

Grace refers to undeserved favor. A core tenet of my faith is that God's love moves Him to give undeserved gifts. According to Scripture, Christ died while we were still sinners. God, our Creator, pursued a relationship with me and afforded me the chance to spend eternity with Him when I cared more about satisfying self than honoring Him. God's grace isn't contingent on my worthiness. Salvation through Christ is the true and ultimate measure of God's love. Grace facilitates our relationship with God and characterizes all the blessings that He gives. God often grants us tangible and intangible gifts and privileges that we do not deserve. That I do not have what I pray for is not because I'm unworthy. Even if our present circumstances are directly related to poor decisions and disobedience, our past doesn't diminish God's love. After years of disobedience, God tells His followers in Israel, "I have loved you with an everlasting love; therefore I have drawn you with lovingkindness" (Jeremiah 31:3). Perfection isn't a prerequisite for God's blessings and, further, no one is perfect!

When we begin to evaluate our worthiness, this action lends itself to self-righteous comparisons. We may wonder why the dishonest salesman receives a promotion. Why the promiscuous woman ends up with the upstanding husband, while the chaste maiden has no suitors. Why do unwed youths celebrate the arrival of their firstborn, meanwhile the couple married for ten years struggles to conceive offspring? While I may strive to live according to Scripture, I'm far from perfect. All of us are. Sanctification, God's transformative work whereby believers become more like Him, free from the influence of sin, is an ongoing process. None of us has "arrived." God's grace extends to all, regardless who we are and what we've done.

When it comes to God's distribution of specific blessings, purpose rather than worthiness is in view. Certainly, there are things that God teaches and waiting builds character; nevertheless, it can't definitively be said that our wait is our fault because we lack fully formed character. We can say more assuredly that the absence of certain blessings is a matter of God's good purpose for our lives. God loves you and me so deeply that He has uniquely fashioned our lives, such that when we yield to Him and allow His plan to unfold, it creates a masterpiece that others can't ignore and the value of which exceeds our present pain and sorrow. Again, I recall Psalm 139:16: "Your eyes have seen my unformed substance; and in Your book were all written, the days that were ordained for me, when as yet there was not one of them." So when we ask, "Why me?" the appropriate answer is because it's a part of God's special purpose for our lives. Why? Because what I'm going through will bring me closer to the Father and allow others to encounter His power.

That what I'm going through can bring me closer to God and encourage others to seek Him is the worst possible outcome for our true enemy and the source of our love misconceptions, Satan. Throughout this journey, I have become increasingly aware of the importance of knowing and recognizing the truth regarding both God's character and Satan's devices. This is because we have an unseen enemy who wishes to tarnish both our relationship with God and our Christian witness. Feeling that I'm unloved and a lesser woman is one of the many mind games that Satan plays. Our enemy knows that he cannot sever my relationship with God, for the Holy Spirit has sealed it.[4] Additionally, Scripture affirms that nothing can separate me from the love of God. Meanwhile, it's possible to have an estranged relationship with God. That is, due to ill feelings toward God and disappointment with His providence, I may cease intimate communion with Him. I may stop praying and reading His Word. I may also abandon Christian community. When these occur, my power and resolve to persevere weaken. Thus, I may make unwise and ungodly decisions in my daily affairs, in turn diminishing my ability to be an effective witness who builds up the body of Christ and introduces others to Him.

Any tendency to withdraw from God, Christian service, and community brings the enemy joy, for he seeks to kill and destroy. In John 8:44, Christ explains that the devil was a murderer from the beginning and that he does not stand in truth. Furthermore, Christ states that the devil is a liar and the father of lies. Not only does Satan seek to destroy, he's a liar. He lies to us about God, others, and ourselves. We likely all agree that lies are destructive.

As I've already shared, one lie about God that Satan perpetuates is that God loves others more than He loves me. Another is that it's foolish to anticipate big things from God because I can't have it all. Satan would have me think that I've reached God's quota of good things and happiness. This tears down my confidence in God and diminishes my hope.

What lies about God, His love, and His goodness are you currently entertaining? Are they driving a wedge between you and God? In considering these questions, think about the frequency of your time communing with God, as well as how often you join others to worship God and learn more about His will. Also, consider how diligently you seek to apply God's instructions and counsel to your life.

When it comes to others, the devil causes me to think others regard themselves as better than my husband and me. He draws my attention to behaviors and exchanges, suggesting that women and couples who've joined the elite parenthood club are intentionally isolating us. Other destructive musings include thoughts that people think something's wrong with me. They're talking about me and everybody wonders why Jumaine and I don't have children. These suspicions, fed by Satan and driven by insecurity, lead to distrust, envy, and, again, disunity. You see, Satan is quite crafty. He subtly uses our despair to cause division within the church body. Not all division is overtly chaotic and severe. Little seeds of discord can carve wedges into otherwise beneficial relationships and keep us from harmoniously working toward a common goal.

Satan uses lies to feed our insecurities. As soon as I recognize one lie that he's feeding me about my self-worth, he feeds me another. Our enemy does his homework. Apparently, he knows I care about my character and integrity, and tries to use that against me. I'll give you an example. One of the talents God has entrusted me with is singing. As a member of my local congregation's praise team, I regularly sing and help lead people into worship. Several times during this journey, I considered withdrawing from the team. Sometimes I found it difficult to sing about God's mighty deeds that I readily saw manifest in the lives of others but seemed to be missing in mine. At other times, I wondered if it was hypocritical to sing joyful praises unto God amid the grave despair and disappointment that I felt. Satan really wanted me to regard myself as a hypocrite.

Fortunately, God grasped ahold of my thoughts. Because God's worthiness to be praised is not contingent on vacillating human emotions, it remains most appropriate for me to sing praises. Contrary to the lie tempting me to step down from the team, my presence on the team does not reflect hypocrisy. Rather, it reveals a will to endure as well as a deeply rooted love for God that hasn't been snuffed by my circumstances. My involvement also reflects God's supernatural power and comfort that allow me to move forward rather than indefinitely wallow in despair. One Sunday, I was especially encouraged when my husband, Jumaine, asked the congregation to give a "sacrifice of praise." Each week, as I rise above negative emotions and sing worshipful harmonies, I render a sacrifice of praise.

None of us should confine our praise to the period that follows the fulfillment of our desires. Rather, we must praise God before we see resolutions and answers to our prayers. I'm especially grateful for my husband's example. Jumaine continues to praise God, serves, and encourages others. He does so with excellence and care even while carrying his own unresolved burdens and unfulfilled desires. Past age forty, Jumaine has yet to achieve the degree of "success" and financial freedom he'd hoped to achieve by now. Wanting to avoid debt, he has to endure things that are falling apart and cannot maximize the space in his home due to projected costs of home repairs and improvements. Moreover, his home has yet to welcome the pitter-patter of little feet belonging to children who call him daddy. Of late, Jumaine has been wanting for friendships wherein quality time together is a priority and he's afforded a social life outside of ministry responsibilities. Meanwhile, people's demanding schedules, changing seasons of life, and likely the fact that he's a pastor have led to lone-liness he seeks to overcome. Yes, Jumaine faithfully serves while awaiting breakthroughs and improvements in his own life. He continually renders sacrifices of praise. He magnifies God rather than his challenges and disappointments.

Don't accept contemptuous musings and ill feelings as your norm. These too can be overcome for a moment, and, in time, perpetually. We must guard our thoughts. In his book, *A Love Worth Giving*, Max Lucado identifies three ways we can ward off unhealthy thoughts. First, we must take our thoughts captive and make every thought obedient to Christ (2 Corinthians 10:5). Second, we can follow Christ's example of demanding Satan and unhealthy thoughts to go away. Third, we must not let unhealthy thoughts in.[5] Instead, we must adhere to Philippians 4:8: "Finally, brethren, whatever is true, whatever is honorable, whatever is right, whatever is pure, whatever is lovely, whatever is of good repute, if there is any excellence and if anything worthy of praise, dwell on these things." We must take command of our thoughts.

Yes, constantly aligning our thoughts to what's excellent and true, and standing strong despite recurring disappointment can be quite difficult. Nevertheless, it's wise to heed Paul's counsel in Ephesians 6:10-13:

Finally, be strong in the Lord and in the strength of His might. Put on the full armor of God, so that you will be able to stand firm against the schemes of the devil. For our struggle is not against flesh and blood, but against the rulers, against the powers, against the world forces of this darkness, against the spiritual forces of wickedness in the heavenly places. Therefore take up the full armor of God, so that you will be able to resist in the evil day and having done everything to stand firm.

Our wait is by no means a passive endeavor. We're engaged in an ongoing battle wherein we must choose happiness, praise, and trust. To resist disparaging thoughts regarding God, oneself, and others, we must choose to fight.

We must make intentional, strategic moves such as diligently reading the Bible even when we don't feel like it. We must choose to listen to and sing songs that encourage and inspire rather than yielding to perpetual sorrow. We must muster strength to come out of seclusion and spend time with others – yes, even spend time with people who presently enjoy the blessings that we desire.

Fortunately, God does not leave us to fight alone. His presence and His Word provide all that we need to stand victoriously and resist the devil's clever attacks. We can rely on God-given strength and resources. Instead of giving up and giving way to negative emotions, armor up! Pull out a weapon from your divine arsenal and fight.

Keep in mind, as Peter also warned, that we need to "Be of sober spirit, be on the alert. Your adversary, the devil, prowls around like a roaring lion, seeking someone to devour. But resist him, firm in your faith" (1 Peter 5:8-9). I have learned to be especially on guard when disillusioned and disappointed. As Peter exhorts, we must resist Satan and his lies, firm in our faith. We must believe that God is who He says He is, that He loves us as His Word conveys, and that through Christ our future is ultimately good. We must remain alert, for Satan also recognizes our vulnerabilities. For this reason, I specialize in preemptive prayer. That is, I recognize my triggers for sorrow and unhealthy musings. When I see potential landmines, I armor up with prayer and biblical truth. For instance, prior to attending gatherings where people are likely to ask about my marital status followed by the infamous questions – Do you have children? How many children do you have? – I armor up and ask God to prepare me to graciously respond. When invited to gatherings where there's likely to be considerable dialogue and anecdotes about children, I armor up. Not only do I armor up, I call in other troops, friends and confidants, to join me in prayer.

After discussing the armor of God, Paul calls on the church to "be on alert with all perseverance and petition for all the saints" (Ephesians 6:18). Often, we may feel alone while waiting. When others join me in prayer and agree to *share* my burden, it not only diminishes Satan's suggestion that I'm alone, but their presence strengthens my defenses. When my strength and munitions weaken, my comrades' presence helps replenish my stores. Solomon rightly observed, "If one can overpower him who is alone, two can resist him. A cord of three strands is not quickly torn apart" (Ecclesiastes 4:12). We fight better when we invite others into the battle alongside us.

We should also note that Peter's warning to resist the devil follows the instruction to cast all of our anxiety on God because He cares for us (1 Peter 5:7). The reminder that God cares for us accompanies attention to the fact that Satan will attempt to overtake us. This opens my eyes to the urgency of abiding in God's Word and making sure that I'm clothed in the full armor of God. That my circumstances have yet to change and I haven't experienced any fertility breakthroughs does not mean that God loves me less than He loves others. This love misconception is a myth Satan seeks to convince me is true. Satan's tactics will bring us to a screeching halt if we're not vigilant. We must cast our cares on God, and continue moving forward. When musings arise that oppose what Scripture teaches regarding God's love and good intentions, stand firm and fight for truth. Further, fight with truth.

Some days are better than others. Armored by God and supported by others who truly care, we live to fight another day. Despite the battle wounds and the artillery smoke that obscures our view, we must choose to fight, knowing that we hold value, we are loved, and victory is ultimately ours to achieve — or give away. I want to win!

Romans 8:37-39–[37]But in all these things we overwhelmingly conquer through Him who loved us. [38]For I am convinced that neither death, nor life, nor angels, nor principalities, nor things present, nor things to come, nor powers, [39]nor height, nor depth, nor any other created thing, will be able to separate us from the love of God, which is in Christ Jesus our Lord.

CHAPTER 5

Questioning God's Promise –
Choose Faith

One of the hardest parts about being in a waiting room for a long time is feeling like the wait may never end. Ever felt this way? In those moments, we wonder how long we'll be there. How do we know that our circumstances will ever change? How do we know that God will do what He promised – or even what He promised at all? These questions require addressing more closely what it means to have faith. Recall, having faith means to trust and align our actions with belief that God is at work and that God will work things out for the best. Faith requires having confidence that God is true to His word.

Let's look at one of the greatest examples of faith in Scripture, Abraham. Abraham followed God's instructions to leave his native country and relatives for an undisclosed land. Although childless, Abraham also believed God when He said, "I will make your descendants as the dust of the earth, so that if anyone can number the dust of the earth, then your descendants can also be numbered " (Genesis 13:16). In Romans 4:19-21, Paul spotlights Abraham's faith. We read, "without becoming weak in faith [Abraham] contemplated his own body, now as good as dead since he was about a hundred years old, and the deadness of Sarah's womb; yet, with respect to the promise of God, he did not waver in unbelief but grew strong in faith, giving glory to God, and being fully assured that what God had promised, He was able also to perform."

Fast forward several years after God first spoke to Abraham about making his descendants a great nation (Genesis 13:16). Even then, aware that God had given him no offspring, Abraham again readily believed God when He specified that Abraham would have an heir who came from his own body (Genesis 15:2-6). At age ninety-nine, still married to a barren wife who was past childbearing age, Abraham again believed God's promise that he'd be a father to a multitude of nations, and that his wife, Sarah would bear him a son. Can you imagine waiting more than twenty years like Abraham? Maybe that's how long you've been waiting. Although Abraham never lost sight of his current reality – childlessness – he still trusted God to deliver on His promise. Ultimately, Sarah did conceive and bear a son to Abraham in his old age, Isaac.

Abraham isn't the only person in Scripture who exhibits faith when his circumstances don't appear to align with God's promises. The Apostle Paul also exhibited confidence in God's providence. One night after encountering an angry mob in Jerusalem, the Lord appeared to Paul, saying, "Take courage; for as you have solemnly witnessed to My cause at Jerusalem, so you must witness at Rome also" (Acts 23:11). When God told Paul that he'd witness in Rome, He didn't mention the rough journey that Paul would face en route. While aboard the ship bound for Rome, Paul and his shipmates encountered a violent storm that lasted many days. Passengers on the ship eventually abandoned hope that they'd survive. Then an angel of God appeared to Paul, affirming his previous vision and ensuring that Paul and the others aboard would make it to land safely. Subsequently, Paul encouraged his shipmates, saying, "Therefore, keep up your courage, men, for I believe God that it will turn out exactly as I have been told" (Acts 27:25). Paul didn't claim to know exactly how they'd survive the storm, but he had faith that they would. Paul believed that one day he'd stand before Caesar in Rome as God said. After surviving the storm and stopping in several cities along the way, Paul eventually reached Rome.

Like Paul and his fellow travelers, our journey may contain rough winds and seas. Mine have come in the form of surgeries, disheartening medical reports, and increasing age, to name a few. Maybe your storm has come in the form of unemployment, broken engagements, relationship turmoil, lost contracts, or academic setbacks. There's every indication that the future we anticipated won't happen. Meanwhile, God encourages us just as He encouraged Paul. We must not minimize timely words of encouragement and what some in the church community may call "God moments": Unexpected occasions that illuminate our perspective on the challenges we face. Take for instance, my personal account of unexpectedly coming across the story of the Shunammite woman as my body healed from surgery. God brought this story to my attention as I questioned my reproductive future.

Throughout time, people gained God's approval for exercising faith. That is, God looked favorably on people who showed confidence in God's word regarding future outcomes. Hebrews chapter 11 reminds us that by faith, Noah followed God's instructions to build an ark, even though he couldn't see any rain coming. By faith, Joseph gave instructions for his remains to be taken from Egypt and brought to the Promised Land. Great things happened throughout history as men and women obeyed God's instructions and remained steadfast in faith even when their present circumstances and God's present instructions regarding the future appeared misaligned.

Growing up in an era where many have made ill-informed, presumptuous faith claims, you, like me, may be more inclined to downplay God's intentions to fill our life with good things. Wanting to steer clear of the "name it and claim it" extreme, we linger on another extreme that says we can never know God's intentions as they relate to our earthly future. While it's true that we do not share in God's omniscience, God does reveal things to us as we commune with Him. If you struggle to distinguish between a self-proclaimed and God-ordained future, seek out God's counsel through His word and prayer. When I first received a notion that God would bless me with offspring, it came during a time when I least expected it. As I explained in Chapter 1, at the time I engaged in a personal Bible study exploring the relationship between Israelite leaders' devotion to God and the nation's plight. I was intrigued by the apparent correlation between each king's devotion to God and the spiritual climate of the nation. The nation's spiritual climate and obedience to God impacted Israel's prosperity and dealings with other nations. I casually read beyond my intended stopping point and stumbled on 2 Kings 4:8-17. In this passage, the prophet Elisha informs a Shunammite woman, who had no children, that within a year she'd embrace a son. As spoken by Elisha, she conceived and bore a son at that season the next year. I earnestly believed that God used this passage to affirm that He intended to bless my husband and me with offspring. Fast forward nearly a decade, and I often wonder if I got it wrong. I second-guess what I genuinely believed to be a divine revelation regarding my future.

The account of Zacharias the priest's response to good news regarding his past petitions, found in Luke 1:5-20, also strikes a chord. When the angel informed him that his wife, Elizabeth would bear a son, he responded, "How will I know this for certain?" At some point in all of our lives, we've probably asked this question. Even as a priest, Zacharias didn't believe the unexpected good news. At times we become accustomed to bad news and disappointment. This, coupled with the difficult facts of our current reality, render it difficult to think our circumstances will ever change. Meanwhile, God stands before us with good news. We must embrace good news and the possibility of miracles. After all, God hears our prayers and responds. We're more receptive to good news when we don't allow the passage of time to diminish our hope. Rather than seeing the passage of time as a greater indication that our dreams will not come true, consider instead that it may very well be proportional to the joy we'll experience when dreams do come true. The passing of time gives us an opportunity to plan a more grand celebration. We can better weather the storm when we believe God's promises are sure to be fulfilled in their proper time.

As I revisit 2 Kings 4, two statements made by the Shunammite woman stand out. When Elisha told her that she'd embrace a son within a year, she replied, "No, my lord, O man of God, do not lie to your maidservant." Maybe she, too, felt that this news was too good to be true and didn't want the prophet to play with her emotions. Maybe she, too, feared clinging to an inaccurate attestation about the future – a future she'd otherwise welcome. The depth of her emotion also comes to light when her promised son later becomes ill and dies. Grieved, the Shunammite woman said to Elisha, "Did I ask for a son from my lord? Did I not say, 'Do not deceive me' (2 Kings 4:28)?" As it turns out, Elisha did not deceive the woman. God returned her promised son to her alive. God did not present an unsolicited picture of a desirable future, only to later crush her heart.

As with the Shunammite woman, God knows our innermost desires. While God did not disclose the details of my path to motherhood, I'm confident that God, knowing my desire to bear children, purposefully led me to what had previously been an unfamiliar biblical account. Thus, like Paul,

I strive to believe what God has communicated to me. I use the term *strive* with the full weight of its meaning. Although my faith waxes and wanes, fortunately, all we need is faith the size of a mustard seed.[6] I believe that I will survive this storm and attain what God ordained.

If you likewise struggle to decipher between a self-proclaimed and God-ordained future, seek out God's counsel through His word and prayer. As I stay before God, various promises in Scripture continue to come to mind and make an indelible impression on my heart and mind. I'll remind you that I have, at times, intentionally steered clear of verses that blatantly speak hope into my circumstances. At the same time, I constantly encounter reminders in God's word that He rewards those who diligently seek Him (Hebrews 11:6). When we delight ourselves in the Lord, He'll give us the desires of our heart (Psalm 37:4). Those who wait on God will not be ashamed (Psalm 25:3). In particular, Scripture shows that God knows fully the sorrow associated with bareness and the joy that offspring bring.[7] Scripture speaks to all of our circumstances.

I'm confident that as you practice the discipline of reading and studying the Bible, you will encounter clear messages regarding how God will provide for you and see you through your current circumstances. God's word affirms our aspirations, re-directs us, or gives us instructions for moving forward. When this happens, we know that God is speaking. Presently, God's message to me is not to abandon hope that my husband and I will one day have children.

Additionally, various answered prayers and circumstances show God's hand in my journey and cause me to cling to the hope that God intends to bless my husband and me with offspring. To begin, after three major surgeries requiring me to consent to surgeons performing an emergency hysterectomy should a life threatening emergency arise and during which I incurred excessive blood loss and subsequent blood transfusions, I still possess all the organs necessary to produce biological children. That is, amid surgeons removing numerous fibroids, and losing large enough amounts of blood to warrant blood transfusions, doctors never had to remove my entire uterus.

Additionally, throughout the years, people I hadn't been in direct contact with for some time randomly contacted me to share dreams and visions. One day I received a call from a friend's mother, sharing that she felt prompted to share a vision she had of me with my future child. On another occasion, my grandmother called from Alabama to share that she had a vision of me holding my baby. Having visited my current home once, she remembered the layout and suggested where we'd set up the nursery when I returned home with my child, so that I wouldn't have to go up and down stairs.

God speaks to us through His Word, prayer, and others. Ask, *Do the conclusions I draw consistently line up with Scripture and what the Holy Spirit is impressing on my heart? Has God clearly said no?*

Following our most recent gut-wrenching blow, a disappointment that rendered my husband speechless, God ministered to him through 1 Thessalonians 5:20-21: "Do not despise prophetic utterances. But examine everything carefully; hold fast to that which is good..." During the weeks preceding this incident, several people shared dreams they had of me being pregnant. Some shared that they saw twins in my future. People earnestly believed that our anticipated good news was within our grasp. Mindful of the dreams and high hopes shared by many, only to be followed by further disappointment, my husband and I began to discount these as products of wishful thinking, precluding us from accepting any positive forecast about our future. All the while, believers are instructed not to despise prophecies. We can simply receive these pronouncements – pronouncements that aren't contrary to Scripture – and leave the outcome to God without passing judgment.

A lengthy wait does not disqualify a perceived promise as true. As author Christine Hoover points out, difficulty and waiting often precede God's activity. She also reminds readers that Samuel anointed David long before David actually became king.[8] Further, David was pursued and his life threatened by Saul. Despite being chased away from his homeland, and a significant passage of time, God's declaration regarding David's future reached fruition. If God hasn't given us an emphatic no, we should not relinquish suggestions that the godly outcomes we pray for will happen. We must abound in faith and never give up hope. Keep praying. Cling to God's promises. As some often say, a *delay* isn't necessarily a denial.

It's reassuring when others share our hope and confidence regarding future outcomes. Nevertheless, not everyone will co-sign our faith claims. We must avoid requiring others to share our expectations, and refrain from harboring resentment toward people who are unable to affirm our hope. After all, God revealed the promise to you and not others. Allow neither another, nor ourselves, to dismiss divine foreshadows of our anticipated future.

Meanwhile, we must allow our actions to follow our faith. Accordingly, the student who failed her last two exams exerts great effort to prepare for the upcoming exam. The father who lost his job six months ago continues to submit job applications and puts his best foot forward during interviews. The middle-aged adult desiring a godly spouse refrains from lowering her standards for a potential husband. The pastor of a small congregation faithfully serves and teaches those who gather each week. The couple struggling with infertility remains sexually intimate, regardless of the immediate procreative outcome.

Considering Romans 4:18,[9] Drew Clyde reminded attendees at the Joint Retreat in 2014 that we must abound in hope even if we do not see signs of God's declarations being true. "In hope against hope," Abraham believed. That is, he continued to believe God's promise although his reality pointed the other direction. I like how commentators Jamieson, Fausset, and Brown describe Abraham's belief. They comment that Abraham remained expectant even when no grounds for hope appeared.[10] We have no problem recognizing what renders our situation impossible from a human vantage point. Fortunately, our promise lies in the hands of God who sees all things, knows all things, and can do all things – except lie.

Not only does God see and know all things, He also has the power to deliver on His promises. Consider Luke 1:37: "For nothing will be impossible with God." In the preceding verses, the angel Gabriel informs Mary that she'll birth a son while she's a virgin. Gabriel also informs Mary that Elizabeth, who was called barren, had conceived a son in her old age. In Genesis 18:14 we read, "Is anything too difficult for the Lord? At the appointed time I will return to you, at this time next year, and Sarah shall have a son." This is the Lord's response when Sarah laughs to herself after overhearing the news that she would have a son the following year, being old.

Similarly, God tells Jeremiah, "Behold, I am the LORD, the God of all flesh; is anything too difficult for Me" (Jeremiah 32:27)? On this occasion, God instructed Jeremiah to buy a field even though the Babylonians would overtake the city. God promised that the Israelites would one day return to the land. Jeremiah demonstrated his confidence in God's promise by purchasing the specified field. After giving the deed of purchase to his assistant, Baruch for safekeeping, Jeremiah praises God: "Ah Lord God! Behold, You have made the heavens and the earth by Your great power and by Your outstretched arm! Nothing is too difficult for You."

Jesus also speaks of God's power to do the humanly impossible. After expressing how difficult it is for a rich man to turn to Christ, His disciples wondered, "Who can be saved?" Christ responded, "With people this is impossible, but with God all things are possible" (Matthew 19:26).

The examples in Scripture of God's power are endless. Another is when the prophet Zechariah in the Old Testament encouraged the returned Jewish exiles to continue rebuilding the temple in Jerusalem. Turning to Zechariah, we read about God promising to return to Zion and dwell in Jerusalem, despite opposition that discouraged hope. In Zechariah 8:6, God's power is contrasted rhetorically with the people's limits: "Thus says the LORD of hosts, 'If it is too difficult in the sight of the remnant of this people in those days, will it also be too difficult in My sight' declares the LORD of hosts." God promised to save and restore His people as only He could.

As I consider the instances in Scripture where God declares that nothing is impossible nor is anything too difficult for Him, it challenges me to cling to God's promises. God makes bold promises amid difficult and humanly impossible circumstances. He promises to produce new life, to restore, and to save. God doesn't make empty promises. He has the power to deliver and intends to deliver. Like Mary, I believe that blessed are those who believe there will be a fulfillment of what has been spoken to them by the Lord (Luke 1:45). Thus we ought to cling to God's promises. May we echo King David's words found in Psalm 27:13-14 (NIV): "I remain confident of this: I will see the goodness of the Lord in the land of the living. Wait for the Lord; be strong and take heart and wait for the Lord."

Habakkuk 2:3 (NKJV)–For the vision is yet for an appointed time, but at the end it shall speak, and not lie: though it tarries, wait for it; because it will surely come, it will not tarry.

Q & A For the Waiting Heart

You may agree it's difficult to remain diligent in prayer when it appears your prayers are going unanswered. Meanwhile, we must trust and obey. Even if it's difficult to "trust," we must obey. Thus, I continue to pray and feast upon God's word. In so doing, God responds to my immediate need for assurance and strength with insights such as these.

Question: *Are You listening?*
How long, O Lord, will I call for help,
And You will not hear? (Habakkuk 1:2a)

God's Response: *I'm working on your behalf.*
Look among the nations! Observe!
Be astonished! Wonder!
Because I am doing something in your days-
You would not believe if you were told. (Habakkuk 1:5)

Our Charge: *Rejoice in the Lord despite the circumstances.*
Though the fig tree should not blossom
And there be no fruit on the vines,
Though the yield of the olive should fail
And the fields produce no food,
Though the flock should be cut off from the fold
And there be no cattle in the stalls,
Yet I will exult in the Lord,
I will rejoice in the God of my salvation. (Habakkuk 3:17-18)

Our Assurance: *We'll survive.*
The Lord God is my strength,
And He has made my feet like hinds' feet,
And makes me walk on my high places. (Habakkuk 3:19)

I have set the Lord continually before me;
Because He is at my right hand, I will not be shaken. (Psalm 16:8)

CHAPTER 6

God's Character and Sovereignty –
Choose Trust

As a child, I longed for the day when I was old enough to make my own decisions and to do what I wanted to do, when I wanted to do it. All the adults who read this book will probably agree that this never fully comes to fruition. There always remains an area of our life in which we must defer to the will, needs, and plans of another. Be it our supervisor, spouse, newborn child, or a professor, someone sets an agenda to which we respectfully yield. It's easiest to yield to the wishes and plans of another when we trust that our submission will produce a desirable outcome. Moreover, when we trust that the person to whom we defer is governed by good intentions, not having our way becomes more bearable. We eventually move past our present displeasure.

As I reflect on God's attributes, I recall why I hesitate to force God's hand (as if I can) regarding conception of offspring. Because I know God has a perfect plan (as already evinced in my life – college, grad school, timing of my relationship with Jumaine, for example), I pause at the idea of pressing God to give us children NOW. This doesn't mean that I do not become impatient. Indeed, I have become both impatient and weary the past several years. As time progresses, rather than demanding that God move now, I petition and press Him for insight into why He hasn't granted my petition. *Why the wait? When will my husband and I finally have children?*

That I do not have the answers to my questions is definitely consistent with God's character. He's sovereign. He reveals what He wants when He wants. It's my responsibility to trust Him and petition Him for immediate contentment, joy, and peace. After all, I'm confident that He wants me to have these attributes now. According to Philippians 4:7-11, one reason we cast our cares on God is to exchange human anxiety for God's peace. Paul also conveys that God provides the strength and grace we need to experience contentment in all circumstances.[11] Moreover, before His departure to heaven, Jesus communicated that He wanted His joy to dwell within His disciples, and that it be made full.[12]

While I recognize that I can make requests rather than demands of God, I also am learning that it's counterproductive to attempt to discern why we're waiting. We may spend countless hours ruminating over questions that God elects not to answer. God, after all, doesn't have to answer to us. I can think back to my childhood. I often wondered why my parents made certain decisions. That they never disclosed the rationale behind the various decisions that I didn't like ultimately did not prevent me from achieving an overall satisfying and fruitful life. Interesting enough, I never asked why when they made decisions that I favored. That we want to know why, ultimately points to our dissatisfaction with God's providence. The real question we're putting before God is: "How can You allow me to be unhappy?" We want God to justify why He's not giving us what we want. If God chose to answer this question, it still may not satisfy or it might make us more enraged for our scope on life and the universe pales in comparison to God's. Our time is better spent focused on things we can actually control and achieve amid unwelcome circumstances.

Additionally, we should be careful about believing every explanation that people offer for why we are waiting. As mentioned in Chapter 4, we may reach false conclusions that cause further despair. For instance, we may feel that God has yet to answer our prayers because there's something inherently wrong with our character that God needs to fix before we can have our blessing. This causes us to become overly critical of ourselves when our flawed character – which will never be perfect this side of heaven – may have nothing to do with the "delay." Of course there is something that we can learn from every challenge that we face, and our character is undoubtedly refined. However, we shouldn't wallow in sorrow over the wrong conclusion that we're not "good enough" yet.

Concluding that we're "not good enough" also can cause us to feel inferior to those who do have what we want. Inferiority breeds insecurity, envy, and resentment. While it's unwise to make comparisons, I'm sure we'll all agree that there are some who live more frivolously and less responsibly than we do, yet they enjoy the blessings we seek. It could be our inherent character flaws and shortcomings have nothing to do with our wait. Then again they may. The truth is, unless God reveals it to us, we do not presently know.

Through experience and Scripture, we do, however, know a lot about God's character. Focusing on what we know of it is essential to pressing forward.

In seeking to understand God's character in my wait, I also have come to recognize that Western Culture has impacted my outlook on life — negatively in some ways. Throughout my life, despite being a follower of Jesus Christ and seeking to live according to Scripture, I've chased the American dream of quality education, a thriving, happy family, and comfortable living. That these are God's priorities is a grave misconception. Additionally, I believe that if you work hard enough, you can attain anything that you want. I value liberty and autonomy. As an adult, I expect to be in control of my life and my own destiny. However, all people, whether we hold to a Christian worldview or not, do well when we come to realize these truths:

- God is sovereign
- Our plans must yield to God's plan
- God desires His due glory.
- God's agenda is redemption and holiness
- God is faithful
- God cares

Above all we must recognize God's sovereignty. According to the *New Oxford American Dictionary*, sovereign means a supreme ruler. As an adjective, the term describes someone who possesses supreme, or ultimate, power. This characterizes God. After all, He created all things. Genesis 1:1 informs us that God made the heavens and the earth. The psalmist writes:

"The Lord has established His throne in the heavens, and His sovereignty rules over all" (Psalm 103:19).
"He established the earth upon its foundations, so that it will not totter forever and ever" (104:5).
"The earth is the Lord's and all it contains, the world and those who dwell in it" (24:1).

Scripture makes it clear that God is all-powerful. Our power pales in comparison. Although God created us in His image[13] with the ability to reason and subdue the earth, we must inevitably submit to His authority and agenda.

Isaiah 45 is a poignant declaration of God's power. Not only does the passage remind us that He is the Creator, it also reflects His ability to elevate and abase whom He pleases. Verse 9 and 10 warn, "Woe to the one who quarrels with his Maker — an earthenware vessel among the vessels of earth! Will the clay say to the potter, 'What are you doing?' Or the thing you are making say, 'He has no hands'? Woe to him who says to a father, 'What are you begetting?' Or to a woman, 'To what are you giving birth?'" Verse 12 adds, "It is I who made the earth, and created man upon it. I stretched out the heavens with My hands." I admit that I've questioned God throughout my journey. If you're like me, this passage evokes a position check and repentance. Our Creator has a greater agenda in view.

Isaiah 45 also reminds us that God desires for the nations to recognize His supremacy and power. One reason He accomplishes amazing feats on behalf of His followers is that all will give allegiance to Him and declare, "Only in the LORD are righteousness and strength" (Isaiah 45:24).

As we navigate life's challenges, we must also remain mindful that God possesses a master plan and sees the big picture. At times I grow weary and impatient with God's timing. Deuteronomy 7:21-22 reminds me that God knows best and accounts for the bigger picture. As in the case of the Israelites, sometimes God brings things to pass little by little so that we are prepared to handle what He's giving us, and such that our blessings won't become an unbearable burden. We read in Deuteronomy 7:21-22: "You shall not dread them, for the LORD your God is in your midst, a great and awesome God. The LORD your God will clear away these nations before you little by little: you will not be able to put an end to them quickly, for the wild beasts would grow too numerous for you." Attainment of our hopes and dreams and acquisition of God's promises don't always come quickly. There's a process that ultimately benefits us. This passage encourages me to trust God's timing for offspring and other unfulfilled desires.

While God causes all things to work together for the good of those who love Him, we must not lose sight that God's divine agenda is at play. Amid the liberties God affords us, He ultimately works to accomplish His purposes. Of greater importance than our own personal sense of fulfillment is the need for us to have a right relationship with Him through Jesus Christ. We find in Scripture that delayed gratification often served a purpose in God's redemptive plan. Take Zacharias and Elizabeth, for example. Scripture says that, "They were both righteous in the sight of God, walking blamelessly in all the commandments and requirements of the Lord. But they had no children" (Luke 1:6-7). When they were advanced in age, God finally informed them that He had heard their petition and Elizabeth would bear a son. Included in God's message was a declaration that "you will have joy and gladness, and many will rejoice at his birth." They were informed that their son would turn many back to God and prepare the way for Christ. The timing of Elizabeth's pregnancy was perfectly aligned to occur just before Christ's advent. Furthermore, Elizabeth's pregnancy confirmed the mind-blowing message that Mary received regarding her own miraculous pregnancy. Elizabeth's pregnancy at an old age served as a timely, living testament that nothing will be impossible with God.[14] John the Baptist's birth not only fulfilled his parents' desires, it served a pivotal, redemptive purpose at a specific time in history.

There's also the instance of Jesus' friend, Lazarus. When Lazarus' sisters informed Jesus of Lazarus' illness, Jesus intentionally waited two days before traveling to see His beloved friends. Within that time, Lazarus died. As a matter of fact, he had been in the tomb four days by the time Jesus arrived. When Martha and Mary each saw Jesus, they said, "Lord, if You had been here, my brother would not have died" (John 11:21, 32). As Jesus witnessed the sorrow surrounding Lazarus' death, He too wept. That Jesus was deeply moved, despite knowing the imminent miracle, reflects God's character. God shares our sorrow, yet He must allow temporary heartaches to accomplish a greater purpose that serves our and others' good.

As the familiar cliché suggests, timing is everything. When Jesus received the news of Lazarus' illness, He knew that his sickness would not end in death. Rather, his sickness was for God's glory.[15] For those who find it unsettling that God uses our hardships to get glory, I pause to convey that as God is glorified, the world recognizes His supremacy, ultimate goodness, and the salvific importance of deference to our Creator. Lives are eternally saved. All who are directly and indirectly involved benefit. Accordingly, when Jesus cried out, "Lazarus, come forth," and His entombed, deceased friend came out, many believed in Jesus. After all, only God could restore life to one who was dead and whose dead body already produced a stench. That Jesus was God incarnate became apparent. Recognizing His power, people were poised to accept His message.

As I endure my own wait and related sorrows, I can especially identify with women in the Bible such as Elizabeth, Sarah, Rachel, Rebekah, and Hannah, who all had prolonged periods without children. We can also learn from these women's experiences that God indeed has a master plan. Furthermore, we see that God is faithful, and He cares. Yes, He has special regard for each of us and forgets about neither us, nor our circumstances.

In a previous chapter, we discussed God's promise to Abraham and Sarah. While this account clearly points to God's faithfulness and the fact that He's true to His word, sometimes I need to know that God is aware of my present condition and hasn't forgotten about me, especially when He seems to be giving "everyone else" the specific blessing that I seek. Genesis 20:17-21:1 is one reason why I remain in awe of God's word and wholeheartedly believe that all

Scripture remains relevant and useful for our lives throughout the ages. These verses occur after Abraham, passing Sarah off as merely his sister, allowed King Abimelech to take Sarah. This wasn't the first time Abraham passed his beautiful wife off as merely his sister to spare his own life while traveling in a foreign territory.[16] God revealed to the king that Sarah was a married woman and warned Abimelech to return her to Abraham to avoid death. God also revealed that Abraham would utter a prayer of healing on behalf of the king and his household, for the Lord had closed the wombs of the king's household while he remained in possession of Sarah. In Genesis 20:17 we read, "Abraham prayed to God, and God healed Abimelech and his wife and his maids, so that they bore children."

Can you imagine how Abraham and Sarah may have felt, praying for someone else's household such that they bore children; meanwhile, they had no offspring together? I certainly know how I've felt time and time again, seeing prayers that I offered on behalf of others answered while mine seemingly remained unanswered. An interesting turn of events occurs in the next chapter. We continue reading in Genesis 21:1, "then the LORD took note of Sarah as He had said, and the LORD did for Sarah as He had promised." That the LORD noticed Sarah communicates that He forgets neither us, nor His promises. Consideration of a situation like Abraham and Sarah's, where it initially appeared that God had blessed another's household at the expense of others also waiting – only for Him to fulfill His promise later – renders God's attention and provision most noteworthy. Our faithful Lord never forgets us. He simply comes through at the most opportune time.

Similarly, after Leah bore Jacob a sixth son and a daughter, Scripture says, "Then God remembered Rachel, and God gave heed to her and opened her womb" (Genesis 30:22). We must remember that God does listen to us. Even as God accomplishes His redemptive purposes, He regards our innermost longings and deepest feelings.

There are other examples in Scripture. Related to the story of Abraham and Sarah, God spoke to her pregnant servant, Hagar in the wilderness and comforted her after she ran, distraught by Sarah's harsh treatment. Hagar rightly identified God as the God who sees.[17]

One of my greatest fears is that because God is sovereign, He will solely give me what He wants me to have and not what I wish. Thus, each fertility disappointment and each suggestion that God has something in mind that I can't imagine causes me to speculate that God has picked out a special blessing for me that will not emanate from my womb. Maybe you have similar reservations regarding God's providence. Fortunately, Scripture and life experiences affirm that not only is God sovereign and faithful, He is a loving God who cares and favorably responds to prayers.

I find Matthew 7: 9-11 reassuring when I begin to doubt God's good intentions. These verses state:

Or what man is there among you who, when his son asks for a loaf will give him a stone? Or if he asks for a fish, he will not give him a snake will he? If you then, being evil, know how to give good gifts to your children, how much more will your Father who is in heaven give what is good to those who ask Him!

Not only does God hear our prayers, He also responds to them with good things. In this passage, Christ uses the example of a parent to emphasize this truth. When it comes to a loving parent, he or she knows what their children want and will seek to give them the good things that they ask for. If mere men "being evil," or given to a sinful nature, know how to give good gifts, of course a holy, all-powerful God does. Mindful that parents do not give children everything they ask for because some things aren't good for them, the same can be said of God. Further, when we pray, we can always expect God to give us what He knows to be good. At times, He may very well give us exactly what we ask. For example, we read in Genesis 25:21 that "Isaac prayed to the LORD on behalf of his wife, because she was barren; and the LORD answered him and Rebekah his wife conceived." In this case, God granted Isaac's exact request.

Hannah also comes to mind when I question if God truly cares — specifically, if He regards prayers for what may be considered life's added bonuses rather than needs. That is, although we may not want to live without these, the truth is we can. For some of us, life's added joys include a spouse and offspring. For others, this may include a job promotion, home ownership, increased revenue, a professional degree, a leading role, or healing from a chronic illness. One could say Hannah had everything, yet she still wanted children. As a matter of fact, Elkanah, her husband, asked, "Hannah, why do you weep and why do you not eat and why is your heart sad? Am I not better to you than ten sons" (1 Samuel 1:8)? Notwithstanding, we read further that, greatly distressed, Hannah prayed to the Lord and wept bitterly.[18] She asked God to remember her and grant her a son. Scripture confirms that God indeed remembered Hannah and granted her petition.[19]

Recall my earlier comments in Chapter 4 regarding seeking to determine the why behind my circumstances. Hannah's story allows us to conclude that, while we may not understand why our circumstances are as they are, at least we know Who is working behind the scenes. 1 Samuel 1:5 informs us that God had closed Hannah's womb. The God who previously closed Hannah's womb also opened her womb, allowing her to conceive.[20] While my flesh is disappointed that God, who is fully capable of changing our circumstances, has yet to grant Jumaine and me offspring, my spirit submits to God's sovereignty. In every circumstance,

God remains at work. As He's closing and opening doors, He's closing and opening wombs. I point this out to emphasize that God isn't passive regarding our waiting rooms. He's actively involved. As Romans 8:28 says, "God causes all things to work together for good to those who love God, to those who are called according to His purpose."

In addition to assuring me that all will be well in the end, Romans 8 brings an important truth to light: The entire earth groans and suffers due to sin. Accordingly, we must not grow frustrated with the providence of our sovereign, faithful Lord as we dwell in a fallen world that will soon give way to a heavenly city where there will no longer be crying or pain.[21] Thus, even though we face heartache and disappointment on earth, the day will come when those in right standing with God will be saved from the presence of sin and sorrow forevermore. Meanwhile, we must remember God's faithfulness. Furthermore, we must not lose sight of the fact that we are already blessed — God has given us plenty to be thankful for. Moreover, we have an eternal hope that transcends our present, temporary disappointments.

As we endeavor to move forward, I pray that we will allow Scripture and our experiential knowledge of God's goodness to remind us that God is at work behind the scenes. God is neither fickle nor passive regarding our waiting. He has great intentions for us all. Our hope quotient rises when we recognize God's sovereignty and trust His character. We must remember that God is sovereign, He's faithful and He cares. We must choose to trust God and His plans.

Lamentations 3:21-23,25–[21]This I recall to my mind, Therefore I have hope. [22]The Lord's lovingkindnesses indeed never cease, For His compassions never fail. [23]They are new every morning; Great is Your faithfulness... [25]The Lord is good to those who wait for Him, To the person who seeks Him.

CHAPTER 7

Benefits of the Barren Season –
Choose Fruitfulness

As I get older, I find that autumn is becoming my favorite season. I love the colorful leaves. Further, the crisp aroma in the air fosters refreshing feelings of nostalgia. Unfortunately, where I live, this season seems to fly by. Life gets busier, and if I'm not intentional about getting out to enjoy this changing season, I lose the opportunity to indulge in the autumn walks and picturesque scenery that I look forward to each year. In a few weeks, all of the trees become bare. Brown, dried-up leaves cover the ground.

Among my least favorite things to behold are bare trees and decomposing leaves. Why does beautiful fall foliage give way to leafless trees? I didn't realize my displeasure was that apparent until a car ride following a snowstorm. I can't recall my exact words as my husband and I drove past bare, seemingly lifeless trees. My husband commented, "You don't like barren trees."

Shortly after, I began to contemplate the science behind why deciduous trees lose their leaves during the fall and remain leafless throughout winter. I had vivid memories of an article my high school biology teacher shared discussing the various plant pigments that become apparent only as hours of sunlight diminish and temperatures begin to drop. During autumn, as daylight hours become shorter, the levels of the green pigment, chlorophyll, decreases. Plant pigments such as chlorophyll absorb usable energy from the sun. As chlorophyll diminishes, other pigments become visible. In time, some trees lose their leaves, allowing them to conserve energy during colder months.

Although the trees look dead, deciduous trees are far from lifeless. This seasonal adaptation allows them to make the most of winter. A period of leaflessness promotes a plant's overall ability to thrive and reproduce.

Through my reflection, it occurred to me that this necessary season of bareness in nature parallels our experiences. In nature and life, we may enjoy colorful, happy moments soon followed by emptiness and decay. We ask ourselves, *Where did life's vibrant colors go? How did winter come so suddenly? Why is my life barren?* Because the natural eye cannot fully behold all that occurs during a *barren* season, without prior learning we fail to perceive the necessity of the fall. The temptation is to stop living rather than wisely use available energy to ensure a glorious spring. We simply go through the motions and yield to the harshness of the conditions we face. Because we cannot presently produce lush vegetation, we ignore the fact that we're still standing and there are things we can do now. We don't have to wait until spring to thrive. During the winter, we can stand as formidable beings, beautifully adorned by ice and snow rather than toppled by severe elements.

Thriving when life seems harshest requires recognizing and maximizing the benefits of our current season. Remember that each season possesses inevitable joys and challenges. Our tendency is to focus on the joys of the seasons we desire – a season of matrimony, a season of parenthood, a season of financial prosperity, a season of relational peace. Meanwhile, we ignore the benefits of our current season and all that we are able to accomplish now. Maybe we remain in the waiting room because God has the benefits of this seemingly barren season in view.

Lacking children, academic degrees, wealth, a spouse, noteworthy status, and so forth, we deem our lives barren. All the while, these are just partial aspects of our lives. There are numerous other areas in which we can and do currently thrive. I recall, when I lacked the amorous relationship and outings with a male companion that I desired, I spent time initiating Bible studies, investing in friendships, mentoring youth, building newly established organizations, and earning two academic degrees. Married, desperately desiring off-spring, God has allowed me to save money, make a voca-tional change, invest countless hours in ministry work, coordinate various retreats and gatherings, and earn a third degree, among other things. Clearly, I've had a productive life. Some may even say that I'm an accomplished young adult. Moreover, I'm already building a legacy within my small-yet-growing sphere of influence. Marriage, offspring, and fame aren't the only means for positively impacting our world and leaving a legacy.

Interestingly, as God adds to my life, I find that some-times doing and acquiring other things that I want requires greater sacrifice. For instance, completing graduate school as a working, unmarried adult was far different than completing my second graduate degree as a married woman. While single, my top priorities were God, work, and school. Although quite social, I knew that I couldn't allow my social life to interfere with coursework. I encountered an unexpected, seemingly unorthodox priority adjustment when I decided to attend sem-inary as a married woman, however. I had to prioritize quality time with my husband. Thus, going out to dinner, cuddling up to watch television on the couch, and going to the movies with Jumaine were as important as completing assignments. Talk about a paradigm shift! I now had to consult with my husband to establish a schedule that allowed me to thrive as both a wife and a student. I never anticipated that juggling act.

Budgeting for two rather than one also presents challenges. When an opportunity to participate in a study tour abroad came along, my husband supported my desire to travel. Nevertheless, he was unable to accompany me on an amazing trip that I longed to share with him. Similarly, when looking for discounted concert tickets, I wondered why one friend kept finding better deals than I did. She commented that it was probably because I was searching for multiple tickets. Who knew that marriage, although a beautiful institution, would make my life more complex rather than perfect it?

I imagine a new season of parenthood will introduce new challenges, considerations, and sacrifices. The spontaneity I now enjoy may taper off for a while. I will have to be more strategic with my time, and more intentional about establishing and guarding personal and family boundaries. After all, work, service, ministry, and social demands won't just abate because our family grows. Similarly, as God adds to your life and allows your season to change, greater responsibility may accompany your newfound joy. As a result, we must maximize our current season and endeavor to thrive where we're presently planted. Enjoy the moment, for it will pass. Hang out with friends, take a trip, start working on the business plan, run the marathon, recruit volunteers for your organization, take another class, submit the grant application, lead the group, serve your community, donate the money.

Difficult, unwelcome circumstances aren't an acceptable excuse for fruitlessness. Throughout Scripture, we see how God esteems industriousness and corrects indolence and passivity. In Jeremiah 29:5-7, God sends this message to the exiled Israelites:

⁵'Build houses and live in them; and plant gardens and eat their produce. ⁶Take wives and become the fathers of sons and daughters, and take wives for your sons and give your daughters to husbands, that they may bear sons and daughters; and multiply there and do not decrease. ⁷Seek the welfare of the city where I have sent you into exile, and pray to the Lord on its behalf; for in its welfare you will have welfare.'

God informed the Jewish exiles that it would be a while before they'd return to their homeland. Rather than being unproductive as they awaited deliverance, God instructed them to live fruitful lives. Even in a foreign, undesirable place, they were to build houses, plant gardens, expand their families, and seek the welfare of the city. In time, restored exiles sang:

Those who sow in tears shall reap with joyful shouting.
He who goes to and fro weeping, carrying his bag of seed,
Shall indeed come again with a shout of joy, bringing his sheaves with him.[22]

Regarding these verses from Psalm 126, some scholars explain, "As in husbandry the sower may cast his seed in a dry and parched soil with desponding fears, so those shall reap abundant fruit who toil in tears with the prayer of faith."[23] We cannot rightly anticipate reaping a harvest if we fail to sow. We must sow, even amid disappointment, dearth, and tears.

For some of us, we are grinding – working hard – while in the waiting room. Meanwhile, there seems to be no return. *What's the point,* we wonder. We're tempted to throw in the towel, to simply sit down and do nothing. We can be tempted to wallow in despondency and watch everyone else be fruitful. Scripture encourages us along a different course, however. Take a look at Ecclesiastes 11:4-6:

⁴He who watches the wind will not sow and he who looks at the clouds will not reap. ⁵Just as you do not know the path of the wind and how bones are formed in the womb of the pregnant woman, so you do not know the activity of God who makes all things. ⁶Sow your seed in the morning and do not be idle in the evening, for you do not know whether morning or evening sowing will succeed, or whether both of them alike will be good.

We must caution allowing what we observe in our present circumstances to determine our willingness to act. We must faithfully steward the responsibilities and opportunities within our present grasp. We're not to simply sit around waiting for the most opportune time to act.[24] Further, we must diligently sow at all times, because we don't know which labor will eventually yield the harvest that we desire.

Remember that waiting *always* precedes reaping. As we discussed in Chapter 1, those of us in the waiting room can be quite time-conscious. We must keep in mind that God's sense of timing differs from ours. We read in Scripture, "with God one day is like a thousand years, and a thousand years like one day" (2 Peter 3:8). Don't confine God to a specific time frame. This may lead to further disappointment. Simply wait and allow God to determine the duration of your current season, all the while keeping your hand to the plow.

As an elementary school student, I was introduced to Groundhog Day. Groundhog Day occurs annually February 2. Each year, my peers and I looked forward to finding out if the groundhog saw its shadow. If the groundhog came out of its hole and saw its shadow, that meant there were six more weeks of winter. On the other hand, if the groundhog didn't see its shadow, spring would come sooner. As if an early spring would expedite the school year. This annual event subtly introduced me to the notion that I could foreshadow – pun intended – the severity and duration of seasons. Over time, I've come to give little regard to Groundhog Day. Rather than focusing on projected timelines of wintery weather, I simply resolve to focus on doing what I need to do to endure winter, however long it lasts, rather than intently looking for spring. Before I know it, I've shed my winter coat, and daffodils have begun to bloom. Focusing on more productive matters, I seem to miss the exact moment spring arrives and leaves are back on the trees. Not only do I get to enjoy spring's new blossoms, my life is more full because I also possess fruit that I wouldn't have if I did nothing throughout winter

Turning to Scripture, in Ecclesiastes, we also learn that there is an appointed time and season for everything.[25] Further, we read that God makes everything beautiful in its time.[26] Although we can neither see nor fully comprehend the totality of our lives, we must leverage what's before us for both our present and future advantage. In hindsight, when we look back on this seemingly barren season, I hope that we will conclude it was actually one of the most productive times of our lives. After all, even our hardships and disappointments are purposeful. Without my lengthy stint in the waiting room and grappling with recurring disappointment, I wouldn't be in a position to candidly write this book. Rather than waiting to write a testimony of deliverance and goal attainment, I seize the present moment to encourage all of us to thrive and live joyfully in our present circumstances. Who knows? My season may change before this book is published. Regardless, I work with the resources, knowledge, and experiences I currently possess. All of us have something to contribute to the world now. There are things we can only accomplish and are best equipped to give in our current season. Find out what they are and get to work! As my husband encouraged our local church congregation during a message series, *Much With Little*, we must stop dragging our feet.

No, busyness isn't a necessary remedy for moving on and forgetting about our circumstances. I'd be lying if I said that I've moved in a direction that steers clear of despair. Moreover, I often cringe when people suggest that "preoccupations" will indefinitely rid people of sorrow. That phenomenon isn't a universal truth. I'm a busy person with a demanding schedule and weighty responsibilities. As a matter of fact, a lot of my activities and "preoccupations" involve serving others. Immersing myself in these has not permanently diverted my attention from the reality that I'm childless, and that childlessness hurts. Sure, there are stints where my fertility challenges aren't at the forefront of my mind. Nevertheless, over the span of ten years, there have been numerous occasions for the grief over this unfulfilled desire to resurface. All the while, by God's grace and strength I serve, work, and produce through the ups and downs. I sow in laughter. I sow in tears.

God, who gives strength to the weary,[27] calls and empowers us to bear fruit even in our current season. Life persists, activity remains even during the winter. We can choose a lifetime of fruitfulness even in a seemingly barren season. May we relish the benefits of our current season and choose fruitfulness.

Philippians 4:11, 13—[11]...I have learned to be content in whatever circumstance I am...[13]I can do all things through Him who strengthens me."

Winter Prayer

Dear God,

Please help me to endure winter. Lord, help me to delight in and take full advantage of all that this season offers. After all, I'll soon be tempted to complain that it's too hot. When I look back on this season at some future point, may I look back with satisfaction rather than regrets. May I conclude that I made the most of winter.

Lord, please help me to thrive rather than spend my days complaining, and fixated on the cold. Grant me grace and strength to joyfully embrace each season with its unique delights and challenges. Your creative works are in play. There's a good purpose for this season; help me to recognize it and rejoice. Lord, as Paul instructed Timothy, help me to remain effective and poised to serve in season and out of season (2 Timothy 4:2).

Even in winter, I must give thanks. I'm grateful for the opportunity afforded me through Christ's atoning work to cast all my cares on You. I'm grateful that You lovingly regard all my prayers and petitions. I'm grateful that Your compassions never fail (Lamentations 3:22). Because You're faithful, I remain standing and can testify of numerous accomplishments in this season and seasons gone by. With or without foliage, my life is indeed full. Lord, I thank You.

Amen.

CHAPTER 8

On The Outside Looking In –
Choose Compassion and Grace

The ups and downs associated with waiting can definitely strain relationships. Although we deal with the pain of our circumstances, people we encounter in the waiting room also have the potential to strengthen our resolve and brighten our journey. Or, they may unknowingly exacerbate our pain and heighten our awareness that we're still waiting. What follows are a few considerations our friends, relatives, and associates are encouraged to consider as they interact with those of us who are waiting — and others.

Since I'm being transparent, there are moments when I just want to speak my mind, burst someone's bubble following an ignorant comment, and make them understand the foolishness and insensitivity of their comments. That I haven't speaks to the magnitude of the Holy Spirit's power working in me. The Holy Spirit controls my tongue and helps me to respond graciously. One of the good things about writing is that it allows me to process my thoughts and ultimately communicate them in a more sober manner. That being so, I'll take this opportunity to share some considerations I wish for onlookers to know. I also invite you to share any that may apply to your circumstances. After all, collecting our thoughts, communicating them in love, and maintaining our composure may be key to maintaining the relationships that we desperately need in the waiting room. Moreover, no tirade will cause us to receive quicker service and to leave the waiting room any sooner. We'll just have more mess and baggage to sort through as we wait, and potentially once we leave the waiting room.

Employ kind, constructive means to engage onlookers and to make them aware of how they can best extend compassionate support and care while we're in the waiting room. Scripture exhorts believers to bear each other's burdens.[28] If our friends, relatives, and onlookers are also reading this book, the following are a few ways they can serve those of us in the waiting room and help make the journey more bearable.

Exercise Social Tactfulness

When attending social gatherings, we anticipate engaging in casual conversation. If we're meeting someone for the first time, there's a familiar list of questions we are likely to ask. *What's your name? Where are you from? What do you do?* Some occasions warrant questions such as these. *How long have you been married? Do you have children? How's business? What's your weekly attendance?* Sometimes we're reconnecting with people after a lengthy time apart. You know, events such as weddings, reunions, and baby showers. People ask — *Are you married yet? Did you come alone? How many children do you have now?* At initial glance, these questions may seem harmless. Meanwhile, for some, these questions awaken our insecurities and greatest disappointments.

First, connections and social gatherings aren't the most opportune time for all personal inquiries. Regrettably, there are certain functions I no longer look forward to. I think long and hard before registering or accepting the invitation. This is because, without fail, someone will ask how long my husband and I have been married, quickly followed by, *Do you have children?* Sometimes there's an awkward silence, as it seems most expect us to be married with children. Some may even pick up on the fact that it's a sensitive issue. On these occasions, I then spend the remainder of the time mentally rehashing my unwelcome reality of childlessness, often while listening to anecdotes involving children and intimations that parenthood is an experience that all in attendance share. Thus, events designed to encourage me and refresh my spirit at times serve as catalysts for downward emotional spirals instead.

Seemingly innocent questions that probe into a person's present conditions and status can be off-putting if you aren't a person's close friend. This being the case, we should give careful thought to the questions we ask. Pick up on cues and avoid assumptions. Sometimes just a few questions are sufficient. *What's your name? How are you doing? Where did you meet? How long have you been in the business?* Accept the introductions and personal information that people readily offer. Possibly, this may be all that they have to share, or all that they wish to share. If they mention neither spouse nor children, think twice before asking. Although we may want to know, we really don't need to know. Consider steering the conversation toward the purpose of the gathering, rather than probing deeper into attendees' personal affairs or the nonpublic, exclusive aspects of their business and organizational affairs — unless, of course, that's the mutually agreed upon reason for your gathering. Elect to leave some things unknown unless the other person initiates disclosure. If your pure motives and concern compel you to know, pray for the right opportunity to ask. Then proceed with compassion and tact.

Further, sometimes it's more polite to withhold comments when someone responds to a question asked in a manner that fails to meet our personal standards or expectations. I recall an unpleasant public exchange when meeting a keynote speaker for the first time. I'm not sure what prompted him to ask Jumaine and me if we had children. However, I vividly recall the appalled look on his face and his disparaging retort in the presence of onlookers, after we stated that we didn't have children. My embarrassment soon gave way to anger. I can only imagine how the conversation may have progressed if his attention hadn't been called elsewhere. Fortunately, this has been the exception rather than the norm when my husband and I share that we don't have children. I share this experience to bring to light that exercising social grace matters. The words we speak and the expressions we make can either encourage or discourage. We should consciously speak words that build people up, are fitting for the occasion, and give grace to those who hear. [29]

Respect Boundaries

Sometimes we're privy to people's struggles and challenges through our familial or close friendship connections. Some people may welcome our listening ear, affirmation, and prayers. Meanwhile, our critical assessments and plausible solutions may be unwelcome, and at times off-putting. Only get involved and offer input to the degree that associates, friends, and loved ones allow. Unless they're at risk of injury, respect their boundaries. Rather than barging into people's affairs, we can let them know that we're available and wait to be invited into their waiting room to the degree that they deem acceptable – or bearable.

No matter how badly you and I want to see our loved ones progress and their problems resolved, sometimes we need to hold back. We can provide emotional support, but we cannot impose solutions. Sometimes our suggestions unwittingly minimize the gravity of our loved one's unique, personal experience in the waiting room. We tell stories and offer remedies that worked for others, assuming that what worked for another may also help our friend. Sometimes these comments trivialize hurting people's experiences and may exacerbate pain. Sometimes we demand that hurting people realize things could be worse, and compel them to be happy. Rather, we should refrain from making assumptions about a person's posture of gratitude and contentment. Gratitude and sorrow aren't mutually exclusive.

Additionally, when someone invites us into their circle of trust further along in the journey, delicately seek to know what they've already tried and considered. Our seemingly new suggestions may insult their intelligence or provide a scathing, familiar refrain that they tire of hearing. Seek permission before barging in with our opinions, suggestions, and counsel.

Some of us may have to beware and avoid feeling entitled to know every detail of a person's circumstances and what they're doing to move past the waiting room. We don't have to know when our loved one is going to settle down and "start a family." We don't have to know why our sister didn't decide to marry him. The couple doesn't have to disclose what parenthood alternatives they're exploring. Neither birth ties, nor familial relations, nor seniority, nor friendship status gives us the right to bypass another's right to privacy. Neither do these require that another accept our critique and suggestions. Some may prefer to respectfully decline our intervention and make their own educated, well-thought-out decisions. Some matters are the sole business of a husband and his wife, a patient and her doctor. Unless we've been given permission to intervene, we shouldn't expect to be directly involved in another's affairs.

We should respect people's right to decline our suggestions and involvement. It's not our place to establish timetables and chart another's course through the waiting room. Accept that all options aren't right for everyone. After all, God has a unique plan for each that doesn't always align with our notion of what's preferable or best. We must allow people to make their own decisions in their own time, without our unsolicited input. Also keep in mind that some things are truly out of all our hands. God is ultimately the only One who can bring resolution.

Listen to Serve

When people do open up about struggles and challenges, refrain from listening to simply appease your curiosity. Listen for the purpose of service. You are now equipped to pray for and provide specific care. We should determine in our hearts that when someone shares a deep concern, challenge or need, we'll do what we can to minister and help bear that burden.

Considering that some struggles are especially difficult to share, it can be most hurtful when people seem to forget or fail to respond to cries for help. This can cause those in crisis to build walls of distrust and to feel alone in their circumstances. I know of instances when people finally opened up about personal issues in what they perceived to be supportive environments. To their dismay, they did not receive the timely follow-up or the outpouring of support that they had anticipated and observed others receiving. In these situations, while their transparency was applauded, it took additional prompting for people to actually follow up and see how they were doing moving forward. On the other hand, they often observed the readiness with which peers rejoiced with others, yet failed to outwardly mourn with them. These experiences can cause people hurting and needing care to refrain from reaching out for help. Not only do they need healing from life's unwelcome blows, they now need to recover from the sense that what they're going through doesn't really matter to others. Neither wanting to burden others nor face the pain of being forgotten, some elect to silently endure their burdens instead. Indefinitely sitting in the waiting room hurting and alone is torturous. It's comforting when onlookers pass by, poised to both listen and to serve.

Both love and service require sacrifice. If we are truly committed to extending compassionate support and service, we must prepare to give something away. Serving others may require that we give resources such as time, energy, food, and money to help meet someone else's needs. I'm grateful for friends who carve out time to call and check up on me. Some have even driven miles from their homes to come visit me, pray with me, and share meals with me following devastating doctor reports. Mindful that fertility woes are only one of my struggles and growing frustrations, some friends have provided tangible support to help lighten the load in other areas of my life. Friends walked alongside me to accomplish fitness goals that, although challenging, were within my capacity to reach. Moreover, they recognized that a healthy, energized body would better equip me to endure my emotional struggles and reduce stress. Imagine my amazement when I saw friends shed tears over MY circumstances – circumstances that aren't an issue of life and death but still matter to me deeply. While wrestling with the fact that at age thirty-six, I have not borne children, imagine my sense of accomplishment, being able to do things physically as an adult that I never achieved during my youth.

We must caution letting our own personal demands and cares cause another's cry to go in one ear and out the other. We must pull out our calendars and notepads, channel our long-term memory, and commit to service. There are various ways we can serve those we know who are dealing with prolonged hardship and disappointment. There are simple ways to extend support that will neither exhaust our resources nor diminish our capacity to meet our own responsibilities. Consider a bi-weekly or monthly check-in call. Rather than simply praying for them on your own, the next time you see them or talk to them, take time to pray together. Send an occasional "thinking of you" card or message. Mark certain "trigger dates" on your calendar. These are the days that are especially challenging for our friends – their deceased child's birthday, Father's Day, the anniversary of their dissolved marriage, Christmas, milestone birthdays, etc. Spend time doing something that the other person enjoys.

Because we do not know how long our loved ones, friends, and acquaintances will remain in the waiting room, we should prepare for the long haul. Numerous forecasts that "this would be my year" suggest that many genuinely thought I'd share their motherhood blessing by now. This, however, isn't the case. Some have remained in my corner for the duration of this longer-than-expected journey. They still call, they still ask, they still encourage. Meanwhile, others have seemingly moved on. Yes, it hurts. I'm learning to thank God for the times that these people were present, and I continually ask God to keep me from taking their present absence personally. It's not that they don't care. Life has simply taken them to new places, in another direction, or placed new people in their path to care for. It's possible that some simply just don't know what to say. They pray as I come to their mind, and elect to stand back and allow God to do what they cannot.

This leads to my final comment regarding listening to serve. Listening and serving, beyond the initial disclosure and throughout the long haul, requires honest communication. We must not hesitate to be candid with others about our capacity to serve. Honestly communicate the extent to which you can provide care and support. Additionally, we must frankly share when we really don't know how to respond to our associates' prolonged hardship. Share that we feel bad because things aren't moving forward for them while things are coming through for us. Ask, *How can I best support you?* Also share that you value their friendship and want to be able to share your good news with them. Accordingly, ask them how you can go about sharing your good news in an acceptable manner. These are questions true friends ask. Sure, these conversations may be uncomfortable. Sometimes, serving others requires us to get uncomfortable. It's my experience that friends' acknowledgment of their feelings and grappling with my pain is far better than them being silent. Honest communication conveys that the hurting person isn't being ignored – that people do, indeed, care. Together, you can come up with a plan to best render support as disheartened people remain in the waiting room.

Nurture Relationships that Transcend Changing Seasons

Being married without children can be a challenging stage of life. Unmarried friends and acquaintance have occasionally made assumptions that I'm spending time with my man, so I cannot hang out with them. Meanwhile, friends and associates with children schedule play dates and plan gatherings with other growing families. I'm not invited to these either. Thus, loneliness is something I've come to experience although I have spousal companionship. As an unmarried woman, I recall determining that I'd be intentional about spending time with friends if God ever provided me male companionship. To God be the glory, throughout our courtship and even in our marriage, Jumaine welcomes fellowship with my friends (now his friends too) and often lets me enjoy time with the ladies.

As I listen to others' stories of feeling isolated and abandoned by friends as their relationships and other statuses change, I feel more strongly about the need to nurture and preserve meaningful relationships that transcend changing seasons of life. By virtue of God's unique plan for our lives, we may not all get married, have children, graduate, and experience career advancement at the same time. Certainly, it's helpful to interact with others who can understand and relate to us in our present season. It's nice to vent, exchange ideas, and connect with people who share our experiences and present struggles. Meanwhile, we must not neglect those who are in other stages of life. After all, these were our friends before we got the job, before we were elected, before we got married, before we had children. They still value our friendship and desire to spend time with us.

Further, when our circles and interactions extend to people in different seasons than ours, we enjoy the benefits of diverse perspectives and experiences. At times, they provide welcome escapes from the demands of our present season and provide the fresh air that we need. Recall growing up. You probably enjoyed hanging with older siblings and schoolmates. We listened intently as they discussed what it was like to be in their grade or in a particular teacher's class. Maybe you enjoyed visiting relatives who just had a baby and playing with your little cousins. We enjoyed Sunday dinners when our parents invited other adults – married and unmarried, college students — and children our age over to the house. All had a good time.

Let's take a look at our friendship circles and calendars. Assess who we're most inclined to spend time with and why. Contemplate whether you're neglecting any meaningful relationships. Are you exerting your greatest effort to spend time with people who are just like you because they're just like you? Leave it to others to determine whether they want to hang out with a bunch of newlyweds, a group of mothers, or a group of bachelors. How about just hanging out with *friends*? After all, categories, statuses, and seasons change. Let's not allow status, position, and stages of life to be the primary factors determining with whom we associate. Keep in mind relationships and friendships aren't one-sided. It's not solely about what's in it for me. We want to serve and extend mutual support. Others benefit when we include them in our lives and we remain a part of theirs.

Now back to those of us waiting. When our friends do choose to extend compassion and service, we must recognize it and convey appreciation. Seek to see people's good intentions rather than filtering every question, remark, and piece of advice through the pain and disappointment that we feel. As earlier discussed, there should be a few trusted people who can candidly speak to us as we deal with the highs and lows of waiting. Recognize that people's steadfast presence is a sacrifice. They are choosing to mourn with us. They seek to genuinely understand what we're going through and how they can encourage us to thrive. They're hoping we don't harbor resentment and jealousy toward them because they have what we want. They earnestly want to say the right thing. They're going out of their way to show that we matter and that we're indeed loved. Accordingly, may we endeavor to lovingly and graciously respond to those who stand outside our circumstances looking in. May we allow them to remain present in our lives.

Job 6:14–For the despairing man there should be kindness from his friend; so that he does not forsake the fear of the Almighty.

The Choice Is Yours

ertainly, the waiting room isn't our preferred location. Notwithstanding, the waiting room is filled with opportunity. Rather than focusing on the disappointment we face and the blessings others enjoy, let's focus on what we can presently achieve and already cherish. Let's commit to making the most of our circumstances. Learn all that we can. Strengthen our minds and bodies for the feats that lie ahead. Use our experiences to help someone else. We *can* be happy. We *can* create precious memories. The choice is ours.

As I write the closing lines of this book – a book difficult to write for numerous reasons, I consider Christ's appeal to God before His arrest and crucifixion. Christ said, "Father, if you are willing, remove this cup from Me; yet not My will, but Yours be done" (Luke 22:42). Jesus was deeply grieved when He prayed,[30] yet He stayed the painful course. I'm beyond grateful that Christ endured the cross. His sacrificial death eternally saves lives. While my experience can redeem none, I'm becoming increasingly aware that a posture of service and devotion to God amid a plight that I'd gladly see pass has far-reaching benefits if I fully engage it. I also recognize and accept that others are inclined to reap the greater earthly benefit than I do.

If, indeed, I'm truly Christ's disciple, this revelation that my present hardship will benefit others should bring me joy. Now, it does. I must admit, however, there have been – and still are – days when I'd much rather birth a child than, as one friend put it, become the poster child for waiting and thriving. This, however, is a part of the Christ follower's mission and legacy. As Paul writes, "If we are afflicted, it is for your comfort and salvation; or if we are comforted, it is for your comfort, which is effective in the patient enduring of the same sufferings" (2 Corinthians 1:6). Contrary to popular belief, this journey isn't all about me, nor is it all about you. Although my longing for offspring persists, God comforts me. Further, He empowers me to encourage and counsel others. This way, we can *all* thrive. We can all live productive, God-honoring lives.

Although I have a desired outcome, I do not fully know how my waiting room account ends. Nor can I control the ending. Meanwhile, God has given me numerous chapters to steward. In writing this book, in continuing in vocational ministry, in preserving friendships, in rejoicing with others, and in helping others amid my own sorrow, I make the most of what's in my hand. No matter the outcome of my fertility journey, it can never be said that I failed to bear fruit.

Similarly, while you wait, opportunities to progress and to serve others exist. What will you accomplish in the waiting room? Who will you serve? The choice is yours. Don't waste the passing time that we're so conscious of. Choose to thrive. Don't allow disappointment and prolonged hardship to be your undoing. Rather, let them propel you to audacious service and achievement. Indeed, the choice is yours. Will you choose to thrive?

2 Corinthians 1:3-4 – ³Blessed be the God and Father of our Lord Jesus Christ, the Father of mercies and God of all comfort, ⁴who comforts us in all our affliction so that we will be able to comfort those who are in any affliction with the comfort with which we ourselves are comforted by God.

End Notes

1 Job 30:27
2 Cloud and Townsend, Boundaries: When To Say Yes, How To Say No, e-book chapter 13.
3 http://www.blueletterbible.org/lang/lexicon/lexicon.cfm?Strongs=G2390&t=NASB
4 Ephesians 1:13-14
5 Max Lucado. A Love Worth Giving Chapter 9 Kindle edition
6 Matthew 17:20
7 See Psalm 113:9, Proverbs 30:15-16, and Isaiah 54:1.
8 Christine Hoover, *The Church Planting Wife* (Chicago: Moody Publishers, 2013), 180-181.
9 Regarding Abraham, Paul wrote – In hope against hope he believed, so that he might become a father of many nations according to that which had been spoken, "So shall your descendants be."
10 Robert Jamieson, A.R. Fausset, A.R. and David Brown, *Commentary Critical and Explanatory on the Whole Bible*, (Oak Harbor, WA: Logos Research Systems, Inc., 1997)
11 Philippians 4:11-13
12 John 15:11
13 Genesis 1:27-28
14 Luke 1:36-37
15 John 11:4

[16] See Genesis 12:10-20
[17] Genesis 16:13
[18] 1 Samuel 1:10
[19] 1 Samuel 1:19-20, 27
[20] 1 Samuel 2:20-21
[21] Revelation 21:4
[22] Psalm 126:5-6
[23] R. Jamieson, A.R. Fausset, and D. Brown, *Commentary Critical and Explanatory on the Whole Bible*, vol. 1 (Oak Harbor, WA: Logos Research Systems, Inc., 1997), 385.
[24] Donald R. Glenn "Ecclesiastes" in *The Bible Knowledge Commentary: Old Testament*, eds. John F. Walvoord and Roy B. Zuck, (Colorado Springs, CO: Cook Communications Ministries, 2000), 1003.
[25] Ecclesiastes 3:1-8
[26] Ecclesiastes 3:11 (KJV)
[27] Isaiah 40:29
[28] Galatians 6:2
[29] Ephesians 4:29 (ESV)
[30] Matthew 26:36-38

CPSIA information can be obtained at www.ICGtesting.com
Printed in the USA
LVOW11s1822310316

481608LV00001B/148/P